F*CK
NAILING
IT

BOOKS BY ANNIKI SOMMERVILLE

How to Be a Boss at Ageing

Motherwhelmed
The B Word

THE HOTBED COLLECTIVE
More Orgasms Please

F*CK NAILING IT

Anniki Sommerville

Thread

Published by Thread in 2022

An imprint of Storyfire Ltd.
Carmelite House
50 Victoria Embankment
London EC4Y 0DZ

www.thread-books.com

ISBN: 978-1-83790-304-7
eBook ISBN: 978-1-80314-046-9

Previously published as *The Big Quit* (978-1-80314-047-6)

To all the women sighing as they set off for another long day at work, wondering if there's something more.

CONTENTS

Chapter Two: Why the Dream Job Doesn't Exist and Why It Doesn't Matter 44

Chapter Three: You Can't Pour from a Broken Fucking Cup: How Self-Care Isn't Just an Instagram Meme.............................59

PROLOGUE

**A Potted History of Women, Work
and Why I Wrote This Book**

Pre-historic times

A woman exits her cave dwelling. She is 25 but has the appearance of a woman three times that age (and if she's lucky she'll die at around 30). She has spent the day washing giant mammoth skins and is now checking to see if they'll be dry enough for the family to sleep on tonight. Her husband is out hunting and her six children are huddled in the cave fighting over the last bit of rat meat (not sure if they ate rats but you get my gist – times were tough). This woman stops for a moment – 'Is there perhaps more to my life than doing this shit every single day?' she asks herself. She stares out onto the horizon; she thinks she can hear the sound of a collective sigh – the sigh of many women echoing from somewhere. The past, the future even? She shrugs. She has the strange sensation that she is the first woman to have ever thought these thoughts but that she will not be the last. A child cries. She shivers and goes back inside.

Medieval times

A woman exits her cottage (constructed out of cow dung and straw which is remarkably effective at keeping out the cold and elements). She is hanging bedlinen out on the washing line while her husband slaughters a pig in the shed. The children are inside eating a stew made out of entrails and are hungrily dipping stale bread into their bowls.

'You need to feed the chickens, wench,' the husband shouts over the screams of the dying pig.

'I already did that, sire. Plus I washed the floors, tidied the rooms, picked wild flowers for your headache tincture and have amused the kids while playing the lute.'

'Well, you'll have to get to market and see if you can get another pig to replace this dead one.'

The woman stares out into the middle distance. She has a restless feeling. It's as if she doesn't enjoy doing all these chores that her husband keeps coming up with but she has no clear idea on what she could do or be. She sighs. For a moment, she can hear an echo of that self-same sigh. She shudders and goes back inside.

Victorian times

A woman sits at a desk. She has wandered into her husband's study and is practising writing with his special quill pen. He is at his surgery today and she is bored because the children are reading quietly and she has done all the day's housework (with the help of the maid and the housekeeper, of course). She picks up one of her husband's anatomy books. She's always been curious about biology but wasn't educated to a high enough level so there are long words that she doesn't understand. She writes on the piece of paper, 'Being a mother and playing the harpsichord isn't enough.' She sets the pen down. She's heard there are women who are trying to get the vote and she thinks about going to one of their rallies. When she sighs it's loud in her ears, almost as if there's another woman standing next to her – a woman from where though? She shudders. Some undefinable feeling runs through her but she can't name it.

Today

A woman stands on the tube staring out of the window on her commute into the office. Her hair is backcombed at the back because she was too busy dropping the kids at the childminder this morning to attend to it. She reaches into her bag and pulls out a dummy attached to her laptop lead and tries to find her charger but it's got tied up with her headphones in a ball of wires. She has three meetings this morning. Then a conference she must attend in a hotel miles away. She tries to read emails as the tube descends into a tunnel. She makes a list of the stuff she should do and sighs – the list gets longer each day. For years, she thought she knew what she wanted – she wanted children. And she also wanted this other thing – a job. But not just any job – she wanted one that challenged her, allowed her to be creative, one where she could hang out with interesting people and learn new things. What happened to that idea? This thing she's doing now doesn't feel like that; it's just leaving her paranoid and exhausted – how can she thrive again? Her sigh threatens to turn into a scream as she comes out of the tunnel again and spots she has 39 urgent emails. The school WhatsApp is pinging and she remembers it's World Earth Day and she's forgotten to buy seeds for the school fair. She is a rusty cart teetering on the brink of a canyon, about to topple over the edge. She has it all, doesn't she? She is the boss of her own destiny. 'You can do this,' says the sign above her desk at work. But does she want to? The sighs reverberate – the sighs of every woman through the ages swirling around and around. She hurls herself into the heaving fray.

Okay, I get it. This is not an accurate depiction of women and work through the ages (there will be a more accurate one later on) but it's interesting that women have spent a lot of time looking for the thing that might give them more meaning in their lives but then when they have found it, they have perhaps discovered that they don't want it. It's also interesting that some women have chosen to abandon work altogether (if they can afford to that is) and dedicate themselves to home-making (and there's nothing wrong with this if it's a choice rather than a sense of giving up because you don't have any idea what work might look like for you).

The reality is that work and our relationship with it changes over time. So, in our twenties and early thirties we may have loved our jobs but then found that once we had kids, and were returning to the office, our whole perspective shifted.

This sense of perspective shift only becomes more pronounced the older you get. So, with age comes a couple of things: a sense that you need to have some synergy between what you love doing and your work, and at the same time insecurities around how relevant you are because work culture is changing at such a rapid pace.

We are old enough to remember fax machines. And the sound the internet made when you were trying to log on and it took three or four minutes to load a webpage.

I did an online survey of over 150 women and then followed up with a selection of these women to get more detail on their responses. I've spoken to so many women in their forties and fifties who feel disillusioned with work and on the back foot. Some of these women had work success in their late twenties and early thirties and then had children (this is apparently a bad idea for women who want a career), and then found that their employer's attitude changed when they returned. Or they returned and just fell out of love with their job. Some were women who stayed at home to bring up children and after a few years out of the office felt out of the loop and no longer sure who they were and what they could do.

'I just don't know what I'm good at,' is a common refrain.

'I feel I have had a real mid-life crisis since turning 40. I think the realisation that you have been working for nearly 20 years and still feeling as if you're not where you should be is hard.'

Or, 'Everything has changed now and nobody wants to hire me.'

Some are stuck in jobs that they hate and this is impacting on their mental and physical health – maybe because the job is just too overwhelming or they hate the people they work with, or a combination of the two.

The 'I won't take shit' phenomenon of older women

Something happens as we get older – on every level we start to take less shit. It is almost as if our crapola detectors become so finely tuned that we recognise right away what's happening in any given situation. This shit detection super skill can be used to our advantage, but there can be some drawbacks too. We can make assumptions about ourselves that aren't helpful or we can be too rigid in our thinking and tell ourselves, 'I can't do that' or, 'they can't do that' or, 'they're criticising me'. This is obviously age-related but while some of these things may be happening, some may just be tied into us being too stuck in our routine ways of thinking or quick to judge.

Fifty-five per cent of the women I interviewed claimed they were often bored and disinterested at work and 15 per cent of said they 'hated it altogether'. Some felt more confident but then claimed they felt jaded, bewildered and unable to keep up (47 per cent). Thirty per cent said they thought about changing their job *every single day*. This is a sobering realisation.

It's normal to have these thoughts but if you're having them all the time then it's time to question your relationship with work and whether you're putting up with a situation that is allowing you to stagnate. Twenty-eight per cent of women said they found younger colleagues 'annoying and they seem to get all the breaks', while 32.5 per cent agreed that 'I feel they know more than me and this puts me at a disadvantage in some areas.' It's not necessarily that we find younger colleagues annoying, it's perhaps more the case that we resent them because we're insecure about our own abilities (seeing them through the lens of our own perceived lacks).

Overwhelm and working mothers

Not feeling confident or clear on what to do next is also common as we get older, as is overwhelm, especially when it comes to parenting and trying to work at the same time. At this moment, I have two young children and am working part time. I can honestly say I have never felt more overwhelmed, and this is with an understanding, supportive employer (I have also worked for less supportive employers and know how it feels to constantly feel under pressure to work harder while trying to stay afloat in the rush hour of parenting that is bringing up little kids). Overwhelm is something that working mothers seem to accept as normal. Working mothers are in a tough position. Childcare is expensive and often not flexible. I have been the breadwinner in my family since year dot and we have months where we barely break even once we've paid for childcare and household bills.

Technology is another thing that can help with this overwhelm but sometimes as we get older we start to feel out of the loop and lack the core skills (or tell ourselves we do). Technology can be super helpful in terms of remote working – it can make life easier in many ways but it also makes us more likely to work 24/7 and blurs the lines between home and work so we are checking emails before we go to bed or while we're with the kids in the park.

And where are the women who inspire us? Where are they?

Thirty per cent of the women I interviewed said they didn't see any working women around them who inspired them. Or if they did see women who inspired them then they were unlikely to be figures in the public eye and more likely to be friends and relatives. *Why?* Is it because the women we see in the public eye who are successful in business don't have the kind of lives that we want?

Is it because women are so hard on themselves that many become workaholic maniacs with their nails bitten to the quick? I would love to be able to say that my female bosses have always been a source of inspiration to me but sadly this hasn't been my experience.

Research has shown that role models are important for women when they're coming up the ranks for three reasons:

- They represent what is possible and help women to see future models of what they could achieve.
- They inspire women to aim higher in terms of their goals.
- They demonstrate the behaviours and attitudes that women need to adopt in order to get there.[1]

Things are changing but for many years the only thing we saw when we read profiles of uber-successful women was a glossy, perfect ideal. We didn't hear about the crying in the toilets or the days when they missed school assembly or the time they screamed at a colleague because they were frustrated. Over and over we read these profiles and they show women who survive on smoothies and HIIT (high intensity interval training) workouts and expensive blow dries but these women don't talk about what it's like to manage companies as women. They don't talk about the guilt which hangs around like a bad smell when you're a working mum or how if one thing goes wrong in the childcare jigsaw, the whole thing collapses. They don't talk about being sleep deprived and going to board meetings with eyes sore as if they've been doused in pickling juice for hours. The cliché of the successful working woman is one where women get up at dawn, work unrealistic schedules, fly around the world and don't even break into a hot flush (older successful women rarely talk about

1 www.forbes.com/sites/margiewarrell/2020/10/09/seeing-is-believing-
  female-role-models-inspire-girls-to-rise/?sh=4ec62c217bf9

the symptoms of menopause or how on earth you lead a company when your hormones are all over the place and you get angry every minute of the day).

We don't see enough women of colour in positions of power or learn about the challenges they've faced in getting there or how they navigated discrimination or racism. A 2018 article in the *Harvard Business Review* revealed that implementing greater diversity is also in a company's best interest (if a business needed any more persuading). Those with the most ethnically diverse teams are thirty-three per cent more likely to outperform their peers on profitability. Those with executive-level gender diversity are 21 per cent more likely to outperform competitors. One clear area that was shown to help women rise through the ranks was having mentors who could guide, and managers who understood the underlying challenges facing senior women of colour (they are more likely to have their credibility questioned and be victims of negative stereoptyping).[2] Without mentors in place or a greater understanding of context then changes are unlikely to happen by themselves (or companies will just pay lip service to diversity).

Business women – why do they often look like robots with bobs?

We cannot be what we cannot see. This is true whatever our background. I just Googled 'business woman' and the images that cropped up were all of white, serious looking women, the majority dressed in grey suits, combined with functional white shirts, and their arms folded defensively. What these images tell us is that women who are in positions of power need to play down their femininity, be very serious at all times and dress in as masculine a way as possible or they won't be taken seriously. It's

2 https://hbr.org/2018/08/how-women-of-color-get-to-senior-management

almost as if all the colour, joy and creativity has been erased. In the market research industry in particular, I rarely saw women I aspired to be. The majority looked a lot like the Google search images and came across as hard and devoid of empathy. This was no doubt what was needed in order to get ahead. When I observed senior women in board meetings they always tended to behave in a subservient manner around men, even if these men were less senior. Even today if you study the covers of *Time* magazine and see how business women are depicted, they look like robots. When I look at a successful working woman, I want to see someone who looks a bit messy. I want her to have a sense of humour (this isn't about cracking jokes on company trips but more about the ability to laugh when things get challenging). I want her to have a bit of toothpaste on her top. I want her to lie on the floor and pretend to play with her children but in fact be fast asleep. I want her to forget things. I don't want her to have a 'morning routine that guarantees productivity'. I don't want her to be so perfect that she never fucks up. I don't want her to do a spinning class in her lunch break. This kind of image of the business woman makes the rest of us feel as if we might as well give up and throw in the towel. It is not a sign of weakness to admit that work is hard and that navigating work and parenthood is hard or that looking after elderly parents and working is hard. We need to see more authentic depictions of successful women so we can weigh up the cost and decide whether (if we are given the opportunities in the first place) we're up for the challenge.

I also acknowledge that I have been programmed not to like women who are successful and so bring this bias when I see women. We see women in a different light from men when they become successful. Sheryl Sandberg, business woman extraordinaire elaborates on this idea: 'Success and likeability are positively correlated for men, and negatively for women. When a man is successful he is liked by both men and women. When a woman is successful, people of both genders like her less.'[3]

It is not perhaps that I don't like women who are successful but it's more the case that I don't want a narrow vision of success – one that is purely about earning a lot of money, having a perfect home and not reflecting the messy, difficult, challenging aspects of everyday work life. I want a woman ripe in contradictions, who shovels Maltesers down her throat and draws willies in her exercise book during meetings. I want her to eat a toasted sandwich from Pret and to cry in the toilets. I want to be able to *relate* to her.

I spent 18 years working in a corporate environment and in the beginning, I firmly believed that working – working hard and earning lots of dosh – was what I wanted. That was what life was about, right? As a Gen X woman I'd grown up in the 1980s when capitalism and consumerism were really having a field day (and are continuing to do so, of course). I rejected my left-wing liberal upbringing and got down with that capitalist vibe. I had a feeling that I wasn't doing the planet much good (because I was selling loads of shit to people who didn't need the shit but thought they did because they were being manipulated into thinking they needed it by marketers like me). I shrugged this off. I also shrugged off the anxiety, the headaches, the crying every Sunday night, the panic attacks and the fact that every fibre in my body was telling me that my work life wasn't working.

When I lost my job, four years ago, I was thrown into a new world of work. It was all short-term contracts and quick turnaround and boasting about your lunch (usually very healthy, with kimchi of some sort) and being continually enthusiastic and bouncy. I was lucky in that I had a nice comfy financial cushion (I got a good redundancy package) but when that ran out, I felt as if I was

---

3 Quote from *Lean In: Women, Work and the Will to Lead* by Sheryl Sandberg (2013, WH Allen)

scrambling to understand what work meant. What did I want? What was I good at? Was I in fact good at anything anymore? I had to earn money. I had kids and a mortgage to pay but I'd also started writing and blogging and was enjoying this side of my life.

In more recent years, I've worked at agencies. I've freelanced. I've been a journalist. I've made podcasts. I've written books. I've gone back into market research to earn money. I've come out again. I've swerved this way and that and, in many ways, I'm still on the journey to working out how to thrive at work. I am aware that work will always be something I must do (the notion of a 'comfy retirement' is pretty much redundant for most of us these days).

I know that I'm not alone in this. A recent study in the US stated that 53 per cent of women said their mental health suffered to 'the point of burnout' because of their jobs, all or some of the time.[4]

This book is a book about women and work. It's a book for women who are not sure what the next chapter of their work history will be. It's for women who have done the same thing for many years and feel as if they're dying. It's for women who sit in the back of an Uber and wish they could trade place with every woman walking past that day (this was often me in my old job). It's for women who have been made redundant and it has shattered their confidence. It's for women who want to change but don't quite know where to start. It's for shy women. And confident women. It's for women who cry on Sunday nights at the prospect of going into the office again.

I've interviewed some truly inspiring women and will share their hacks and tools to not only survive the world of work but also to *thrive*. I've also included some diagrams because I have spent so much time writing PowerPoint slides that this is how my brain works now.

4 www.surveymonkey.com/curiosity/cnbc-women-at-work-2021

One of the biggest learnings about work which has taken me a long, long time to realise is that *it's important* but not *so important that it should dictate your life.* It really is that simple. If you want it to be the most important thing in your life then fine but if you don't, if you want to just work and not have to spend every single waking minute worrying about it (as I have in the past), then that's fine too. The other thing I have learned and will talk more on later is that there will always be stress where work is involved and that it's impossible to find a job that doesn't involve this. What isn't good is when you dread work, when you wake up with that dread, when you get heart palpitations at the thought of it, when you hate your job and your colleagues and fantasise about setting their heads on fire.

It may be, however, that working in a job to pay the bills is a necessary evil. If it is then I hope that you can slowly side-step into something that is more rewarding. Sometimes we don't have any choice because we simply need money, and that needs to be acknowledged too. However, if you are in the position where you can look for alternatives, even if they are incremental improvements, then it's still worth doing in terms of preserving your mental and physical health.

We women who are in our forties and fifties knew work before it became bean bags and brainstorms and blue sky thinking and beers on a Friday and chai tea latte in the kitchen and sushi breakfasts. We also know that sometimes these things are bollocks if they are used to camouflage a toxic work culture and bad people management. There is a clarity that comes with getting older – a recognition of what matters and what doesn't. I'd rather have a great HR person than a bean bag any day.

Midlife brings a wealth of opportunities – it is a time to seriously assess where our life is headed and we can either continue with behaviours that no longer serve us or we can decide that we need to change course. This applies to our relationships, our health, our body – and to our jobs. We will be working for longer and the most important thing to consider is to think about eighty-nine-year-old you, looking back on these years, and how you are going to feel. Will you be proud of the action you took? Or will you still be sighing?

We women have been sighing for a very long time now when it comes to our work lives, and we owe it to ourselves to better understand what we want so we can make the next chapter of our lives truly great. It is about embracing a work life that is not relentless, not about 'nailing it', 'bossing it' and '#winningatlife'. It's about rejecting the notion of being always on and always productive. Because that's just exhausting and bollocks, isn't it?

A quote that perfectly encapsulates the 'don't give a shit' feeling that grows as we age is from one of my favourite writers, Elizabeth Gilbert:

> We all spend our twenties and thirties trying so hard to be perfect, because we're so worried about what people will think of us. Then we get into our forties and fifties, and we finally start to be free, because we decide that we don't give a damn what anyone thinks of us. But you won't be completely free until you reach your sixties and seventies, when you finally realise this liberating truth – nobody was ever thinking about you, anyhow.[5]

Let's not wait till our sixties and seventies to turn around our work life. Let's do it now instead.

---

5 *Big Magic: Creative Living Beyond Fear* by Elizabeth Gilbert (2015, Bloomsbury)

CHAPTER ONE

How Women's Work Expectations
Have Changed Over Time

First off, may I please add a caveat to this chapter? I am not a historian. I loved history in secondary school but mainly the bit that involved drawing cartoons of Henry VIII and his various wives, and creating an authentically aged Magna Carta by roasting an old piece of paper in the oven. We also stuck our history teacher to the chair with Super Glue (no lie – I went to a south London version of St Trinian's).

This history of work and women is written from my own perspective.

The old days of work

Women haven't been working all that long.

I mean they have been working, of course they've been working, but they haven't always been paid for that work. Many were cleaning, bringing up children, entertaining their husband's boring friends through cooking exotic foods, sewing, mending and gritting their tiny, feminine teeth when the men drank port and discussed politics and the important stuff (like work) and they had to go and play the harp with the other ladies and fight the urge to tear their own heads off and scream.

It is no wonder that many women ended up in sanatoriums. They didn't just end up there because they felt suffocated, they also ended up there if they didn't live up to their husband's expectations of what a good wife should be (compliant, likeable, pleasing, quiet and with not an ounce of controversy in her delicate, lovely body).

And the women who didn't work in 'proper jobs' (whatever that means) were middle class and upper class women – and not all of them were weighed down with domestic chores because they had servants of course. Working class women always worked in whatever way they could to support their families but it wasn't work that was celebrated or paid well and so it often went unnoticed.

The first female MP was Constance Markievicz and she would have cut a lonely figure with all the 'DODs' (dusty old duffers) who inhabited political spheres at that time (to some extent they still do though many have had their teeth whitened and take regular showers now). DODs are the ones sometimes spotted asleep in the corner when there's a debate going on inside the Houses of Parliament or they're chanting 'HEEEERRRREEEE HAAAARRR' or something incomprehensible while drinking brandy from a hip flask. But I digress – is there a female equivalent to the DOD? If so, send me some examples on a postcard please.

Women and working during wars

When the first and second world wars broke out then women entered the workforces en masse because society needed them – what with all the men being off fighting and getting killed. So, women got jobs in the factories and made bombs, boots and uniforms. This wasn't about job satisfaction or feminism. It was pure necessity. It's unclear whether women enjoyed it but I'd suggest that many found it a pleasing alternative to cleaning the toilet and trying to make dinner with tiny portions of food because everything was rationed. Oh, wait they were doing that too because they were working and bringing up a family and children and surviving wars. NEWSFLASH. It's nothing new, the whole 'domestic admin' thing, it's just that there seems to be more admin now because we micro-manage so many aspects of our and our children's lives.

Post-industrial times and women have grown their presence at work

Post-war and since the industrial revolution, women have become a growing part of the workforce. There are a few reasons why this has happened but one of the key ones (in simple terms) is that we have more jobs now that don't involve heavy labour and blasting materials with massive fire guns (sorry, I know that's not the technical term, but the things you see in old documentaries where a man is wearing a metal helmet and there are sparks of fire flying everywhere and you worry that he's about to set himself alight if he isn't careful) and more jobs that involve sitting down in offices, typing on computers and replying to a relentless amount of Slack/WhatsApp/email messages. One of the greatest barriers to women working was lack of education (it was only in 1947 that Cambridge University fully validated women's degrees, for example) and so more women being educated, plus the changing nature of work, meant that more women worked.

The superwoman of the 1980s – she had shit to prove and goddamn it she proved it

Fast forward to the 1980s and a new concept of women and work emerged – the concept of the *superwoman*. It's funny because it feels old fashioned now – the idea of being super human and able to do absolutely everything – parenting, work, relationship, social life, sex life, home, cooking, and entertaining. But no, wait, there is still that vibe, isn't there? If we look at magazine covers, women are still tasked with having a great career, being an entertainer, parent, sexy person, and looking amazing. The terminology has changed so she's no longer known as the *superwoman* but is simply a *woman*.

Thankfully, one of the *very* few positive things that came out of the recent pandemic is that the *woman/superwoman* vibe disintegrated and women decided, and are still deciding, that trying to do everything and be everything was a stupid idea. The only women who achieved everything were very rich and outsourcing 90 per cent of what they were doing anyway.

Shirley Conran, author of the 1980s' handbook for modern women, *Superwoman*, said famously, 'I would rather lie on a sofa than sweep beneath it', and this was something that perhaps got lost in translation. The women who could afford to pay someone to sweep under their sofas were happy enough (and had time to write bestsellers) but that left many of us sweeping under our sofas, trying to sit on them and write bestsellers at the same time (and something had to give, right?).

Let me flag up something about privilege here. It's an obvious point but needs to be made.

Wealthy women and work

I am privileged in that I own my own property (but must pay the mortgage each month, which means I can't prance about making bobble hats). It has taken me a long time to realise that the women I've aspired to be have been more privileged and were either born into money or had wealthy husbands. I was basically comparing myself to women who were out of my league. This is quite common with women as we're raised to compare our status with other women, often on a visual level – that one is more attractive, that one is less attractive – but also on an achievement level – that one has a bigger loft than me, or that one has a tiny front room (you think I'm joking, but many of the women I know still do this even when they don't realise they're doing it – comparing the square footage of their homes with other women and feeling smug).

A note on wealthy people in case you don't always clock them right away. They may look similar because they don't wear top hats and have cravats anymore (some of them do but they're likely to say things like, 'Where do you summer?' and 'What's your family name?'). If they are male, they may wear bright chino trousers and be called Tarquin Zanzibar-Jones. They don't worry so much about work or maybe they do but the point is they have connections so can do whatever the arse they want. I remember chatting to a woman in Somerset once a few years back (I was thinking of moving there but then realised that it was mainly wealthy people who did this and that these people didn't necessarily need to work or get into London on a regular basis) and she said, 'Why don't you get your husband to buy you an art gallery and you'll have something to do?'

I'd seen this woman around the village where we were staying, and thought she was inspiring. She had that 'Luella Bartley/ Notting Hill in the noughties vibe' going on – the Land Rover, grey whippets, the Barbour jacket and messy hair in a bun. She had croissant crumbs around her mouth but could carry it off – you know the type. *I wonder if I can be like her*, I'd thought to myself. The realisation that her husband *had* bought her an art gallery to keep her amused shattered those aspirations. If you open many broadsheet newspapers you will read columns written by women like this and wonder at how they manage to do it all. The answer is they have rich husbands or were born into wealth. They outsource everything. They say they're busy but it's not busy. It's not getting a sweat on because you are running home from work and want to see your children for two minutes before they go to bed and you then must get back on your laptop to hit a deadline that evening (and this is easy, I know, compared to lots of other women who are working three jobs at the same time). I am not judging these wealthy women or the outsourcing but just be mindful of piling too much pressure on yourself.

Work is a necessity for me. I pay the bills. I'm not going to start singing some rallying Beyoncé lyric here but, basically, I depend on me. Work is not something I dabble in because my pilates class finishes at two and I have an hour spare. It can't be a hobby. I am also super-privileged in that I have usually had a choice in terms of what kind of work I do. I have worked in a fast-food restaurant, as a cleaner and a greengrocer, and at times this has provided me with a good point of comparison. The first job I got in market research felt luxurious because I could sit down. Many women are stuck in low-paid jobs and feel trapped. Too many women struggle to find well-paid work, let alone finding work that is interesting to them. I am incredibly lucky to be able to turn down jobs I don't want, although I am now at the age where ageism is creeping in and that brings a lot more insecurity.

Does work need to be the *be all and end all*?

Women have only been working for a relatively short amount of time and it has only been far more recently that the concept of enjoyment and work came into play. Enjoyment and work made things trickier. It muddied the waters. Post pandemic many of us are looking for work that not only pays but also makes us feel good about ourselves. The fact that we've been confronted by our own mortality, have spent oodles of time at home, have perhaps realised that the pace we were moving at was unsustainable – all these things have resulted in women re-thinking their relationship with work. Age also impacts on the way we feel too.

The older we are, the longer we've worked, the more jaded perhaps we feel and we're also less prepared to compromise.

The first stage of my work life which started in 1998 and went through to 2017 looked a bit like this:

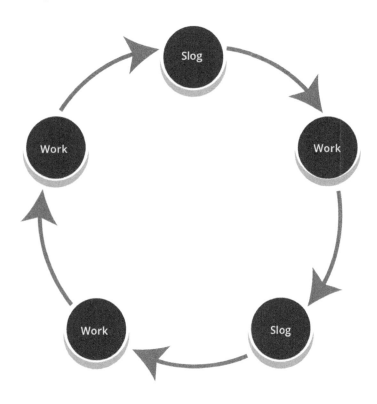

It could also be represented in a more positive way like this:

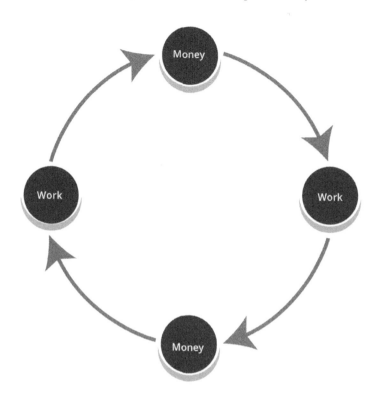

We don't see work as a source of pleasure or fun

Women often have a hard time 'having fun'. Speak to any mother and she will tell you that her head is so full of obligations and house admin that she finds it almost impossible to play with her kids and has turned into the harridan who just constantly tells everyone to put on coats or tidy up mess or brush teeth. We also find it hard to have fun in bed because we are so programmed to service others needs above our own. I wrote a book[6] about orgasms with my friend Lisa Williams (it's in the Resources section at the back) and there is a clear connection between women not being brought up to believe they are entitled to fun in any aspect of their lives, be that work or sex. The narrative that's been fed to us is always one of duty and while I don't expect you to have orgasms at work, it would be nice if it was pleasurable at least some of the time, right?

I worked in market research; it was hard, long hours but it was well paid. I felt isolated. I was a managing partner but was under stress every day. I felt as if I was living in Sheryl Sandberg's body and didn't like it there (I'm sure she likes being in her body but it wasn't comfortable for me). I was pretending I was a corporate hot shot and had the power bob and the shoulder pads (no joke, I owned about six blazers and wore them religiously to every meeting) but inside I was dying. I was self-medicating with pain-killers just to get through each day. I was also trying desperately to get pregnant but hadn't seen any link between work pressure, feeling isolated and my fertility (I'm certain work stress played a part in my struggle – not the only part but a part nonetheless). So here is what that middle part looked like:

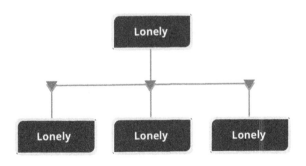

---

6 *More Orgasms Please: Why Female Pleasure Matters* by The Hotbed Collective (2019, Vintage Digital)

But that wouldn't be strictly true as it wasn't always lonely. It was when I was travelling back from focus groups very late at night in a car driving down the M5. It was lonely when I went back to my fancy hotel room and watched infomercials for tummy muscle exercise machines because I had jet lag and couldn't sleep. But I also had some great friends. I bought a lot of clothes. I managed to buy a small house. It wasn't all bad. It was in fact what many women look for when they seek a job. It gave money and status. It gave respect. Then I took voluntary redundancy. The company I'd been with for eighteen years wasn't doing brilliantly and I was one of many who took redundancy. I had become a mother at this point and my work life could be best represented like this:

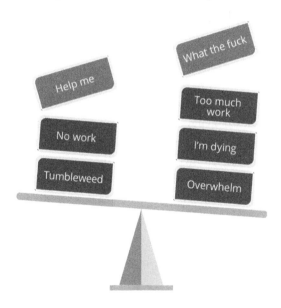

It's useful to look at the past and your feelings and emotions when it comes to work as it helps clarify what you do want from work now and how things have changed. The point of this book is to give you advice on understanding what you want from work moving forward.

One of the big learnings for me when I looked back on my work history was the realisation that work had always been my main narrative and that I derived all my meaning from it. When I hated it, it meant I hated myself. This is something that has changed as I've aged. Work is no longer *who I am*. It is just one facet. And believe me, once you realise this, it is truly bloody marvellous and makes everything feel much less exhausting. Stuff like family, relationships, fitness, home, travel, poetry, reading, films, sex and all these things are important too.

It's also impossible to excel at everything at the same time. It just isn't possible. There is always a compromise happening somewhere and once you realise this, it makes things much easier.

One of my good friends said to me recently, 'I am going to focus on parenting for a bit now and take my foot off the work pedal for a while.' I loved this idea – she wasn't suggesting that she hadn't been parenting before but more the fact that her kids were small, they were highly demanding and it was impossible for her to throw all her energies into work and achieve her professional ambitions while also tending to these children. There are a million reasons why raising kids is hard when you're working (and I'll touch on these later) but if you make a decision to coast while they're little then that's not a bad thing and could take some of the pressure off.

Why striving for perfectionism is bad

Newsflash: You cannot be good at everything. It simply isn't possible. Throughout your career, you are likely to find yourself dwelling on stuff that went wrong or some negative feedback you got from a colleague. As women, we set ourselves incredibly high standards – this is because we've been raised that way. We must look perfect, not step out of line, our houses must be perfect and we must be good mothers and likeable, easy, clever colleagues who never lose our shit or want to murder the people we work with.

The truth is that you will become more aware of your strengths and weaknesses as you get older and you will see that there are similar patterns in terms of the areas where you excel and the areas where you struggle. It's always good to grow and try new things but sometimes it is also worth checking in with yourself to see whether you are setting objectives for yourself that are simply unachievable. Nobody is perfect. You will make mistakes. Men are better at shrugging off the mistakes and getting on with their day. A friend at work recently said to me, 'Why don't you see the good stuff you do in colour and the things that went wrong in black and white? That way the good stuff stands out more and helps you remember what you're great at.' I like that advice because I am otherwise guilty of only looking at the stuff that went wrong each day and then getting trapped in the continual drive to be perfect. The most important thing I say to myself each day is, 'I will do my best today.' It's cheesy but it is all we can ever do.

Why finding meaning in work is important, unless it isn't important to you

In the late 1990s when I started work I didn't really show off about my job. People didn't understand what market research was and thought it was chiefly standing with a clipboard stopping people in the supermarket to ask them whether they ate a certain brand of crisps (and this is what some market research is about and I did this later and it was awful because nobody stopped and I felt as if I was invisible, so now I stop whenever I see someone doing this self-same thing). If a market researcher in a supermarket had stopped me at the start of my career and asked me what I thought about my job and what work meant, the conversation would have gone like this:

Market researcher: Excuse me but can you stop for a minute so I can ask you a question?

Me (harassed, with a foundation line around my neck and too much blusher because I only learned how to apply make up in my early thirties): Sure, but make it fast. Actually, hang on I can't talk to you because I work in market research so I'm not allowed.

Market researcher: This is just an illustration for a book though. It's an example to show what work used to be about in the 1990s.

Me (looking confused): Okay, ask away. I'm not sure I can help you though.

Market researcher: What does work mean to you?

Me: Ummm… it's a drag.

Market researcher: But more than that, what does it mean? What do you associate with it?

Me: Being in an office or travelling and feeling tired.

Market researcher: Okay, but what meaning does it have?

Me: I'm not sure what you mean. It doesn't have meaning. What are you trying to get at?

Market researcher: Are you saying that it doesn't define who you are?

Me (pondering): Yes, I guess so. I mean I don't want 'market researcher' to go on my gravestone, if you see what I mean.

At this point I would walk off and wouldn't think any more about it and would probably buy some blue cheese spread and then get a packet of pants upstairs even though I didn't need them and then a large bottle of wine because I was going through a phase of drinking wine every evening and didn't get hangovers back then.

The point is that now, some of us, maybe the older ones (but it can happen at any time in your career really), want a job that gives us meaning. We spend so much time at our desks that we don't want all that time to be dedicated to something meaningless. It might not be possible to make that change right now but we want to make it eventually. We want to at least start moving in the right direction.

Just as work has changed over time for women, so we can change our relationship with work.

It's not just older women who are looking for meaning in work. A 2018 survey in the US revealed that nine out of ten employees were willing to trade a percentage of their lifetime earnings for greater meaning at work.[7] It also revealed that if people find more meaning in their work then they're likely to work harder so it's in employers' interests to keep every age group of workers engaged.

Try the exercise below to help you identify when work felt more meaningful and rewarding.

Looking back at your work history, what do you notice?

Draw a line on a piece of paper and then branches coming out identifying highs and lows of your work life.

Looking at the highs, what made your work more rewarding at that particular time?

Really think about the times when you've enjoyed work and looked forward to it – if you can't think of this, think of a specific task that you enjoy instead.

Was it the kind of work you were doing? The place? The people? All three?

What did your ideal day look like when you were really enjoying work?

Now look at the low times. What do they have in common? Think about the task, the place, the people and so on. Why were these so dissatisfying back then?

---

7 https://hbr.org/2018/11/9-out-of-10-people-are-willing-to-earn-less-money-to-do-more-meaningful-work

What can you learn about your own work history so that you can build more meaningful work for the future?

Fill in the blanks in this sentence: I am happiest at work when… with… in a place that is… and I am mainly doing…

As with many things in life, there will be times when you want to hit pause and tread water and times when you are up for a big change and hitting the accelerator, or even just speeding up a bit with more purpose in your tank.

All this is to come. Buckle in. Get your shoulder pads out and give them a dust off. No, ditch the shoulder pads – we don't need them where we're heading.

Be More Alice Cooper and Dump the People Pleasing

When I was a little girl, I once sank my teeth into a wooden doorframe because my father wouldn't buy me a teddy bear. It was a particularly fetching bear – you could zip off his fur to reveal pyjamas underneath and I was obsessed with having one. We lived in a small one-bedroom flat in Hamilton, Ontario, in Canada, and I'd creep down at night and open the door to the flat downstairs (this was in the 1970s so maybe there was no lock – I don't know) and steal the bear from my neighbour's daughter. I coveted that bear. I had an effective, single-minded approach to getting what I wanted. I then went through a phase of biting people I didn't like. I was very loud. I was sometimes so loud that my parents didn't know what to do with me to calm me down. Then at about nine years old something kicked in. The something that kicked in was societal pressure – the pressure as a girl to be 'nice'.

If you're in your forties now, then it's likely you too had this pressure and it's interesting to think about how it's impacted on your relationship with work. Do you still strive to be nice? Do you want your work colleagues to be your friends all the time?

I'm not saying that biting or stealing stuff is okay, but I remember frequently being told that my more exuberant behaviours were not acceptable as a girl. It wasn't nice to be single-minded and go after what you wanted. Or to jump up and down with a pair of tights on your head (one of my other tricks was to hold my breath until my face went bright red – this was something I did to get attention when I couldn't bite, jump and down with tights on my head).

Forget being nice from now on please

While it's true that we need to have a handle on our emotions and not hurt others, it's also not helpful to prioritise *niceness*. It can really hold us back. And if you want to learn more about how not expressing your opinion can hold you back, I'd recommend you read *Radical Candor: How to Get What You Want by Saying What You Meansw*, by Kim Scott. In it, Scott talks about how to manage people while retaining your authenticity. Women need to reprogramme their brains so they stop believing that being likeable is the key objective at work.

Being nice made me afraid to express my opinion or to stand up for other people. It also made me unlikely to call out unprofessional behaviour. Even today there is a battle in my head between wanting people to like me and saying what I really feel. I'm more aware of it now though, and try to say things that make me uncomfortable.

I recently had a female boss and was talking to a friend about her and the friend said, 'Yeah, I've heard she's ruthless.'

I thought for a moment and then agreed. Later when I considered this comment, I realised it was incorrect. This boss wasn't ruthless. She was simply a woman who didn't care about whether people liked her and so said exactly what was on her mind. I had to challenge my thinking and accept that this more direct style was in fact inspiring (there were other aspects that weren't so inspiring but I did learn some skills from her directness, as she was always clear on what she expected).

This niceness meant I went three years without getting a salary review because I was worried it would rock the boat. I got upset and couldn't sleep when I got signs that somebody didn't like me. (It was impossible not to like me as I did everything to make other people feel better. I laughed at their jokes. I bigged them up in meetings.) In a meeting, I'd often offer someone a sandwich that

I wanted. I would always be the one hunched under the board room table trying to find the plug for the company laptop because nobody else could be arsed to get down there. I would have stayed a nice doormat until I was loaded into my coffin, if two things hadn't happened to me: children and redundancy.

These two things created a revolution inside my body. First off, I was so fucking tired. I also didn't want to spend time away from my children doing something I hated each day. I needed to work but I had to have some level of satisfaction with this work. The other thing was I realised that I couldn't trust any employer to have my best interests at heart.

The little girl who had laid dormant for so long, the one who had stuck her teeth into the shop doorframe, came to life.

It was like that classic rock video where Alice Cooper screams 'NO MORE MR NICE GUY!' with a snake wrapped around his neck. I had this tougher personality that had big hair and bad attitude and didn't give a shit quite so much.

This is one of the many great things we bring to work when we age: the realisation that we don't care about being nice anymore. It doesn't mean we must be hateful bastards, it simply means we can express our opinions more, be more authentic and not ruminate quite so much on what the fallout will be.

It means we don't offer up our sandwich or slide around under the table trying to find the charging point (or we may do but not as a first reflex in every single meeting).

So, if you're still stuck in that social conditioning, think back to the girl who liked to make mud pies and fart noises. The one who guffawed and spat at the same time while eating rhubarb crumble. The one who peed her pants on the trampoline.

Then say, 'I am sorry that I strangled you and replaced you with a nice, compliant robot. I want to get you back in my life please.'

Then realise that she was there all along.

Be more Alice Cooper.

CHAPTER TWO

Why the Dream Job Doesn't Exist and
Why It Doesn't Matter

Flashback to 1987.

Big perm energy.

Frosted gold lipstick.

Go West are in the charts.

'What do you want to be when you grow up?' my careers advice teacher said. 'Have you got any ideas?'

She impatiently chewed the end of her pencil – probably because she had 40 more interviews to conduct that day with girls with frosted lipstick drenched in too much deodorant.

'I think I want to do something in fashion maybe?' I replied.

The problem was that my education (through magazines and popular culture) was chiefly centred around being attractive, getting married and having children. I didn't see women around me who were ambitious or single-minded (there was one girl who wanted to conduct autopsies but she was decidedly odd – not that it's odd to want to do that, but she was).

Anyway, we were sitting in this teacher's office, me on a plastic orange chair and her behind a desk stacked with folders. She was wearing a brown suit and wooden earrings. I remember the wooden earrings because this was one thing *I knew* about myself – one thing I knew with great certainty. *I would never wear wooden earrings*. I was 15 and just about to commit one of the biggest career mess-ups of my life – jacking in my A-levels and running away to live in Amsterdam with a musician who was ten years older than me and had been in a relatively famous Goth band (this is a whole different story – a story about why I have always been drawn to older men and expected them to sort my life out rather than sorting it out myself).

Can I be famous please?

Whenever I thought about my future life it was shaped chiefly by Impulse deodorant adverts and music videos. I wanted to be beautiful and have the kind of perm that framed my face but didn't make me look like a poodle. I wanted to have a pop star boyfriend or ideally a couple of pop star boyfriends who would fight over me in public. I would spend much of my day posing for photographs for *Just 17* magazine and going to bars and being photographed by the paparazzi when I came out. I wanted to be famous. I had been educated by the predominant culture in the 1980s that being beautiful and snagging a rich man was the way forward. If this couldn't be achieved then a career in a glamorous sphere would be the next best thing (making it more likely to snag a rich bloke too). My favourite fantasy was one where I was working in a photographic studio (doing *what* I wasn't clear on) and then a pop star would come in to have his photo taken and would be so overcome with my attractiveness that he'd drop everything and get down on one knee and we'd then get married and the dream would morph into the Aha video with Morten Harket – the cartoon one – and we'd dance off into the vague but ultimately glamourous future together. I knew better than to tell the teacher this as I'd witnessed her taking down another girl, when she'd said she'd wanted to be an actress, and it hadn't been pretty. We needed to be realistic. We needed jobs that paid well and would allow us to get on the property ladder. It was a confusing time – we were being told that we should follow our dreams and be authentic (my favourite film director was John Hughes who made iconic films like *The Breakfast Club* and the narratives were always about *being yourself* and *not bending to conformity*) but in school it felt as if we needed to grow a pair and be responsible and pragmatic (and push down any unrealistic ideas about our futures).

When I squinted into the fuzzy, far-off future world, truth be told, I had no bloody clue what my work life would look like.

'Why don't you take a secretarial course and get some speed typing skills?' Mum said when I told her I was worried.

I then went and did a speed typing test at an agency to see if I could temp and failed miserably because the ticking noise that the computer made made me so nervous my fingertips started sweating and skidding around the keys.

BUT WHAT DO YOU WANT TO DO? the bossy voice boomed inside my head.

This is the ongoing theme for many of us growing up. Primary school is when we feel the world is our lobster – we're going to be doctors, police women, dentists, ballerinas, astronauts, vets. Then we got to secondary school and we start to realise that maybe we're quite shit at some of the subjects required to get into those vocations. Then we suddenly find ourselves being shunted out into the world, unsure what to do next (not all of us but this was my story).

'At least if you can type properly,' Mum had said, 'you can get a dependable job. You'll never be unemployed anyway.'

I pictured myself wearing a tight pencil skirt and glasses (again the imagery taken from an Impulse deodorant advert I'd seen where a frumpy woman metamorphosed into a sexy girl on a motorcycle with one spritz of cheap scent). I pictured myself marching about in said pencil skirt and the two pop stars fighting over me, and me rolling out of a bar with the paparazzi following my every move.

One of the key reasons that women don't apply for senior roles is the fact that they don't feel they're qualified enough to do so. A 2014 survey in the US revealed that young women tend to be more rule-bound, and they are brought up to believe that following the rules is important if they want to get ahead. This has the knock-on effect of them thinking they can't 'wing it' or be flexible when it comes to applying for jobs (they must meet *all* the criteria so it isn't worth aiming high).[8]

What did I want? Why was it so hard to visualise? Why was my idea of work so vague and difficult to pin down and informed by adverts? Also, why were we expected to have a clear idea of our future professional lives at the age of fifteen? And why, if this was the case, were we never exposed to a variety of different occupations and told that there were more jobs out there that didn't involve marrying pop stars? (Which, let's face it, only a very small minority of women can do – and it is a job – but it is also beyond your control as it's simply about the cheekbones and breast-to-hip-to-waist size ratio you've been blessed with.)

I've thought about this a bit and realised that the reason is I just wasn't exposed to women with interesting and diverse jobs while at school. It comes back to the importance of role models and ensuring that women see a diverse range of female examples early on. Jennifer Siebel Newsom's 2011 Sundance documentary *Miss Representation* features lots of insights around why women are not represented in positions of power. One of the stand-out quotes was by Marian Wright Edelman, Founder and President of the Children's Defence Fund who said: 'You can't be what you can't see.'

My mother had a great job working in medical ethics but I had no clear idea about what she did all day because we never spoke

---

8 https://hbr.org/2014/08/why-women-dont-apply-for-jobs-unless-theyre-100-qualified

about it, and so from an early age I struggled to visualise what my professional life would look like. She was also permanently exhausted as she was working full time and had three children (and for some of that time was a single parent). I remember thinking that work was hard, that it was impossible to combine motherhood with work too. It also didn't feel as if women shared their struggles back in the 1980s – it was frowned on to talk about how hard it was to work and bring up children. One positive is that we do talk about it more now – but there is still a lack of practical solutions to the struggle.

The career advice I wish I'd been given

I wish the career advisor had put me straight. It wouldn't have been that hard. She could have perhaps said something like the following:

> Listen up, bad perm girl. You need to wake up and smell the coffee. You're going to be working for your entire adult life. The reason you're struggling to define what you want is because all the narratives about young women that you see are about being sexy and finding a hunky bloke to support you. This isn't going to work for you as you *need money*. It also isn't going to work because you look like Nancy Spungen (Sid Vicious's doomed girlfriend – Google her and the likeness between us is uncanny) and have legs like a rhino. You need to really dedicate some time and energy to thinking about what you want from work and then take the first step.

Was I the only girl who thought that a handsome prince would scoop me up and take care of me so I wouldn't need to work at all?

I also wish, like really wish she'd told me the following:

And here's one really useful thing that you can write down in your little exercise book – which I notice is covered in doodles of Morten Harket – I want you to despatch any notions of cadging a *dream job*. I want you to stop fantasising that there is some job out there, some career that is so well suited to you that you'll spend the next 20-odd years feeling sad because you haven't found it. Yes, some, a small minority, may know what this thing is and find this thing and you may read about them in articles and feel sad *but* most people don't find their dream job and the reason they don't find it is *because it doesn't actually exist.*

The notion of a *dream job* that there is something we should be doing that is so fulfilling and in tune with our core skills and will make us feel authentic and full of joy every moment is a not helpful. It's not helpful because it's just like the idea of a *dream man* or a *dream family life* or a *dream friend.* It's unrealistic and it puts too much pressure on ourselves in terms of our expectations around work and makes us feel down because we're doing jobs that don't feel perfect all the time.

I spoke to Emma Gage, coach and founder of 'The Wild Ones', a coaching business that helps women reach their full potential, who is also an expert in helping women pivot into new careers. She said:

> I think the pursuit of the 'dream job' is wrapped up in the feeling that everyone should have a driving passion for what they do and if they don't, then they're someone who lacks ambition. The causes of this myth are multiple – social media, the trend of toxic positivity and the need to find gratitude in everything, profiles of women who appear to 'have it all'… it all sets the bar very high.

Now there may be some of you reading this and thinking – hang on, I actually do have my dream job thanks and I'm really happy and think you're on a bit of a downer about work right now because I present my authentic self each day and feel appreciated and satisfied and couldn't want for more.

And I say to you, well done (and what are you doing picking up this book because you don't need it?). I also get that there are women out there who know from an early age what they want to be – a doctor, a pilot, a pop star's wife – and these women go out and achieve those things and are happy (or may realise that their dream job wasn't quite what it was cut out to be because they married Phil Collins and got dumped via fax – I'm showing my age here and excuse me for the references to pop stars who no longer feature in our day-to-day popular culture).

The concept of a dream job is damaging because it presents a professional life that is perfect and without challenges, changes or obstructions.

Emma adds:

> The reality is more like, we're all messy works-in-progress, even those who look as though they've 'made it'. We only hear and feel the messy realities going on in our own heads and lives, versus seeing the polished, final article of other people's lives. We all need to spend more time growing our awareness of what lights us up, rather than looking outwards for inspiration. One person's dream job is likely another's hell. Too often we confuse our values with the things we're good at. You can do a job you're good at and that someone is willing to pay you for and it can still suck the life out of you. I don't think the dream job concept is about the job at all. It's 100 per cent about your own mindset.

So, looking back on your school days, did the fact that you believed in the concept of a dream job influence how you felt about work? Are you still, 35 years later, looking for a dream job and finding it elusive?

Maybe that is because it doesn't exist for everyone. Or maybe that's because you just haven't been shown enough examples of women with different, interesting jobs. Or maybe, like me, you lived with your head in the clouds and believed that you'd marry Morten Harket one day. Maybe you believed that you didn't have what it took to get the job that you dreamt about.

Social media amplifies the idea of a dream job

In the old days, back in the 80s, magazines were our main sources of influence, and films – for me the films *9 to 5* and *Pretty Woman* were very influential. In fact, whenever I enter an office to this day I find myself humming the theme tune to *9 to 5* and many media students have written about the damage Richard Gere and Julia Roberts inflicted on young women and their aspirations (propagating the damaging myth that the secret to happiness is bagging a rich man). As Emma points out, fast forward to today and social media continues to peddle the myth of the dream job. When you scroll through your feed it's littered with affirmations from life coaches and career gurus who all exclaim the following:

LIVE YOUR DREAMS.
YOU ARE MAGNIFICENT AND CAN BE YOUR
AUTHENTIC SELVES.
FOLLOW YOUR HEART AND WEALTH WILL FOLLOW.

One thing I have learned is that *you can earn a lot of money doing something you seriously hate*. In fact, you are quite likely to earn money doing stuff you hate because it's hard, it requires long hours and slog, and not everybody wants to do it. When women hit their forties this pressure to *find the thing that is your dream job and do it* is a real burden (and there's a sense that the clock is ticking and they may go to their grave without ever finding that thing).

One of the most common things women tell me when I'm talking to them about work is: 'I know I want to do something now the kids are a bit older and I know I have to work but I just don't know what the thing is.'

WHAT IS THE THING? WHAT IS THE THING? WHAT IS THE THING?

When Gen X women were growing up we were told that jobs were pretty much for life. So, the pressure to 'get it right' was enormous. If you are going to be doing the same job for 50-odd years then you better be certain that it's something you love. The thing is that isn't true anymore and hasn't been for some time. The reality of work now is change. Trying out new things. Pivoting. Freelancing. Short-term contracts. The people who excel in this new world of work are comfortable with change, or pretend they are. There are downsides of this too. Instability. Uncertainty. Not knowing what each work day will bring. The positive side, though, can feel quite liberating because it means that as long as you have a growth mindset, as long as you aren't too rigid in your thinking you can try different things. An example of this is that I used to work in market research but started doing some work on a well-known blog at the same time. I then managed some social media (I was never trained to do this but enjoyed creating my own content on Instagram). I am currently working part time managing social media and PR for a childcare app. The only thing that has made this possible has been my change in mindset. I no longer tell myself 'I'll make the move when I have learned all the skills I need.' Instead, I've made the move and then taught myself on the job. I've had to use a lot of affirmations to keep me going on bad days. Sometimes I fuck things up. Overall, however, I have moved and am moving in this more flexible, shifting world (and I never believed this was possible because I'd always done the same thing day in, day out).

On one level, this means less job security, more anxiety, more heart palpitations because you're having to continually adapt to new circumstances *but* on another it's a liberating concept because it means if you don't like the job you're doing in this moment, then you may be able to sidestep into a job that you like more.

One thing that I've found useful (when I can't work out where I want to head to next in terms of my job but know I'm not happy) is to identify what my '*shit job*' would be like. Through identifying that, I manage to get base-level clarity on what I want from my next job (and I've only been comfortable with even saying the phrase 'next job' relatively recently as I stayed in the same job for over 18 years despite not enjoying it for about 70 percent of the time).

So, here's a list of what my shit job would include:

- Toxic people who are competitive and don't help one another.
- Meetings which never achieve anything and are more about attendees showcasing their fluency in whatever marketing terms are de rigueur that week (pulling out quotes from a book that is trending on Twitter to make everyone feel on the back foot because they haven't had time to read the book).
- A boss or bosses that people fear because it's not clear what the boss expects or these expectations change dependent on the wind direction.
- People crying in the toilets daily (it's okay to cry in the toilets, in fact it's useful, but not every day).
- People being signed off work for stress daily.
- A commute which takes so long that you have time to listen to a podcast, write a debrief and reply to all the school

WhatsApps from the last ten days. A commute which means you must set off for work when you arrive home.

- A commute that is so long that you never see your children/partner/family/home.
- A commute where you listen to Radiohead and feel as if they really are articulating your inner world right now.
- A commute where you fantasise about death as a positive alternative.
- Lunches sat eaten hunched over your laptop and then being told off for having crumbs in your laptop because you've had to eat all your lunches while working.
- Working on tech platforms which are supposed to make work easier but become the barrier to getting anything done because each time you try and enter information into them, the boxes change shape/your computer crashes.
- Friday night beers on bean bags.

Now it's your turn. What would be on your list? Once you understand what your parameters are and what constitutes a really shit job, you'll be better able to identify the key criteria for a not-so-shit job (notice I didn't use the word 'dream' but it might be your dream to have a slightly less shit job, right?).

And if you're in your shit job right this moment (and are reading this in the toilet with your feet up against the door and maybe crying but maybe also doing some deep breathing to calm yourself down because every person and aspect of your job is driving you mad), well all I can say to you is *I see you*. I see you and I am hugging you now – hugging you even though you are on the toilet and my sleeves are dangling on the floor a little and it feels inappropriate.

Things will change. There is a point where you simply can't take any more. If you have reached this point (and your list of things you hate is long and it makes you frown and even cry when you think about it) then you need to start working on your CV and you need to get on LinkedIn.

Once I had the list of my shit job attributes, I was better able to articulate what my not-so-shit job would be like.

Again, here's my list (and you can make your own):

- Colleagues who you can actually work with and won't create untold drama.
- A boss who is clear in expressing what they want and is empathetic and inspiring.
- Interesting work that feels challenging but also some work that is a bit mindless so you can get on with it.
- A short commute.
- Some working from home.
- Employees encouraged to take lunch breaks and leave on time.
- No enforced socialising of any kind.
- A focus on getting work done rather than how many hours you've worked.

Can I make a note here on 'hybrid working'? Post pandemic, this kind of working has become the norm and this is in many ways a good thing. It has meant that more people are allowed to work from home and there isn't the obsession to always be working in an office. There are, however, some downsides to each environment and there is a lot of work that needs to be done around ensuring that work from home doesn't feel isolating, overwhelming (with a tendency to get caught up in domestic admin and childcare) or that people who work from home aren't passed over for promotions and pay rises because they're less visible than those in the office. These are exciting times in terms of *where* we work but we need to also look at *how* we work in these spaces too.

I need flexibility. I need empathy. I need somewhere I can cry when I'm having a bad day. I need not too much enthusiasm. I need food that I understand and is reasonably priced because the choice of food available in modern workplace restaurants confuses me – and I sometimes long for a cheese and pickle sandwich on white bread and a cup of tea. Writing down the shit job list has helped me understand what it is I do want. And the thing is, this can change. We no longer have this idea that we stay in the same job until we collect our carriage clock and get a signed card and maybe a Colin the Caterpillar cake and a hundred quid behind the bar.

Don't get lost in somebody else's definition of success

Sometimes it's hard to know what we want when the traditional definitions of success fed to us by capitalism are all about having more stuff. It's hard, very hard, not to get lost in that stuff. I am massively lucky in that I own a house. I bought a flat when I was in my thirties and working like a bastard. This isn't possible for many and so I have to remind myself that I'm already super privileged. However, the house is small and the kids share a room and it seems that I am surrounded by neighbours and friends who have bigger houses and the obligatory loft extension and kitchen with the swanky island in the middle and they go on holidays abroad and have expensive cars. There are days when I look at these people and feel massively jealous. However, I then have to slap myself around the face and say:

> Anniki, do you want to work every hour that God sends? Do you want to be on your phone, literally hunched over with your teeth grinding up against one another because some arsehole has sent you an email at ten at night and you're now in the midst of some awful work drama?

Now it's not always true that money and success require arseholes mailing you late at night but in my experience there is always some sort of compromise. I know that the loft extensions come with a lot of hard work and stress. I was the person who lived that life for a long time but couldn't do it anymore. Hence, I won't have the fucking loft extension.

You need to ensure that you truly know what you want and what you're willing to compromise.

Emma adds the following:

'When you know your "why?" and you understand your core values and what drives you, you can make aligned decisions about the kind of job you want and how it fits into your life. The lies are that it will be easy, we'll love every minute of it and that the rewards will just come. That's no one's reality. For most of my clients (and for me in the past) their "peak experiences" in a job have been the times when they worked hard to achieve something, or to overcome something and were proud of their efforts. It feels fulfilling and you feel good about your growth. It's never about ease.'

So if you are at a phase of your life where you are up for working hard and really pushing the pedal to the metal career wise, then that's fine but also don't feel crap if that's not what you want.

Phrases I Fucking Hate

Here are some phrases that are used all the time in work scenarios that I simply think are bollocks and make us feel even more under pressure:

- Nailing it.
- Bossing it.
- Owning it.
- Leaning in.
- Boss life.
- Mum boss.
- Let's do this.
- Winning at life.
- Smashing it.

Alternatives we could use instead to make ourselves feel better about work:

- I've done an okay job today.
- At least I didn't fuck up today.
- I got it done.
- Done is better than perfect.
- I'm tired but I did it anyway.
- Tomorrow is another day.
- I want to go home and have a hot bath please.
- Let's finish this when we can all think straight.

CHAPTER THREE

You Can't Pour from a Broken Fucking Cup: How Self-Care Isn't Just an Instagram Meme

Don't accept being 'tired shamed'

I had a boss when I was in the cut and thrust of my market research career (a female one) and she used to be ultra-competitive about health.

'I never get a cold,' she said to me when I came into the office with a tissue glued to my nose, sniffing and shuffling sadly. 'I never get jet lag either.'

This boss used to get on a plane to New York, type emails all the way there and drink coffee, get off the plane, and after a couple of more doses of caffeine, work until the following evening. I worked out it was 36 hours sometimes that she was working without rest.

'I don't need sleep,' she'd say on the odd occasion when we travelled together.

I thought of that Bon Jovi song, 'I'll Sleep When I'm Dead.'

I thought about how Bon Jovi meant it in a good way – as if they wanted to ride about in the desert and have a laugh and be bandits and have massive hair but this boss meant it in an entirely different way. She wanted to fill all the time she saved not sleeping with work. This was her idea of fun.

She never said the words, 'Sleep is for pussies', but that was the underlying discourse.

In her presence, I felt weak. I had a body that didn't respond well to punishing flight schedules. My eyes always disappeared and felt like pickled onions, stingy and sore. If I got up at five every day and went to bed at one (which was typical back then), I got bad headaches and wanted to cry.

'Jesus, you look like shit,' a male colleague said one morning at six thirty as we checked into Heathrow Terminal 3 to fly to Berlin to do groups on a new ice-cream positioning.

'Cheers,' I replied and helped myself to a giant handful of cashew nuts marinated in business-man urine that were placed on a bowl at the business class bar.

He was cut from the same cloth as my boss. Colds were for wimps. If you were good at your work then you ignored the signals from your body telling you to stop working, you simply kept on going.

This notion that impossible levels of stamina and working 24/7 is aspirational still exists. If anything, it became more pervasive as we got used to working from home during the pandemic and found the boundaries between work and personal life come tumbling down. Suddenly it was normal to be reading work emails while watching TV in the evening. Or doing a work Zoom meeting at 7.30 p.m. The people we often look up to seem to have impossible work schedules and rarely mention the levels of compromise that must go on to make work happen. We may laugh when we see a child popping into a live TV interview, but the reality is that having children at home and being forced to work at the same time is possibly the most stressful dynamic of all. It is exhausting to feel stretched in so many directions.

If you are someone who really gets off on working impossible hours then fine, but it's important to check in with yourself and see how much of your drive is linked to what you think society is telling you about success. How much of it is down to reading ridiculous profiles of people who get up at three so they can work out and eat bircher muesli? As we get older, we get better (it is hoped) at seeing the myths that culture create around work. Of course, we need to work but we don't have to work ourselves to death and if this is what your employer expects of you then you need to start looking elsewhere (and often it is the most senior people in the business who set the example – it's hard to slack off when you know your boss is working all hours of the day and night).

A quick aside – stress makes you smell bad

Apparently when you're under stress you secrete 30 times more sweat than normal. Your apocrine glands located under your armpits omit a special sweat that is richer in proteins and lipids (I'm not joking. Google it) and so even if you don't like your body, even if you believe that pushing it to the edge of performance is good, well maybe just think about what you're making your colleagues endure long term.

When I got a senior position, and was promoted to managing partner, my boss gave me an article entitled 'How to be a Corporate Athlete'.

'It's really useful,' she said looking me up and down, 'It'll help you stay on top of things.'

I never read it (and apologies to whomever wrote it but the title alone makes me want to lie on the sofa, eat Doritos and watch Netflix). The suggestion was that you needed to become an Olympian to survive the business world. You needed to have stamina. Relentless drive. You had to ignore your body, grit your teeth and knuckle down like Tom Cruise in *Mission Impossible*.

It was a macho idea. It was born out of the idea that we were put on this earth to work like bastards and then die.

The 'give me five minutes, I'm checking something' mindset

This diagram represents that trap we get into when we are forever in a state of checking. It's limbo. It's like the feeling you get when you are looking for your glasses but they're sat on top of your head. It's uneasy. The checking. Throughout the day, it builds up so that by teatime the checking has got so bad that you're hunched over your phone and not coming up for breath. It's not healthy. It's not good.

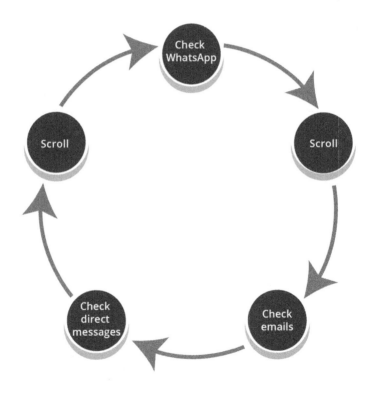

We know all this and yet cannot tear our sore eyes away. If I get locked into this mindset for too long (and it tends to happen to me midweek if I've been working solid for a couple of days and cannot switch off) then I start to get a twitch in my eye and my vision gets blurry. My body is clearly saying to me: *Get the fuck off your phone you imbecile*! I am slowly, slowly getting better at listening.

This phone addiction is rampant across age groups. Apparently 35 per cent of people think of their phones first thing when they wake up, with only 10 per cent thinking of their significant others. The same study revealed that that 44 per cent of 18–24 year-olds have fallen asleep with their phones in their hands.[9]

When the Goddess of Work made us (and she must have loved work because she set the world up so we would all have to do a lot of it), she gave us fingers and toes and soft, fleshy bodies and a brain that was good at avoiding wild pigs and caves with bears hiding in them but was not designed for continually hitting the refresh button on your email. Our eyes were designed to check the horizon for crazy dinosaurs running towards our families (I get muddled but am sure there were some dinosaurs about, or is that *Jurassic Park*?). Our eyes were not designed to stare at a screen for hours and hours and then the minute we get up from that screen to grab a phone and walk to the toilet with it and then come back to the screen, only to get home and watch another screen until we go to bed.

We are not robots (even if the media depicts some working women as such) and we need to remember this.

We have soft fleshy bodies that get sore necks and backs and fingers. The older we are the more unnatural this whole being on screens thing feels (because we remember the days when we used Filofaxes and wrote things down and met people face to face and didn't do everything via an interface). It's important whatever age we are to be mindful of technology and mindful of how our body reacts to it and how it shapes our behaviour towards others.

---

9 www.psychguides.com/behavioral-disorders/cell-phone-addiction

Reading too much into emails

If I sit opposite to you and say, 'That PowerPoint chart you wrote was great but I didn't understand what you meant when you used the phrase "menopausal hierarchy"', that's no reason to freak out, right?

If I type that message in an email and send it to you at 9.45 p.m. when you've just cleansed your face with your lovely Liz Earle cleanser and have written a short gratitude list and are clambering into bed, about to listen to Matthew McConaughey reading his autobiography on Audible (it's very good and I didn't just listen to it because I liked his voice, okay?), well then it is likely to keep you awake and you will no doubt ruminate on the feedback.

Did she not like my use of 'menopausal hierarchy'?
Why did she not understand it?
Am I out of touch because I am actually menopausal?
Is the word hierarchy right?
When she said the PowerPoint was 'great', what did she mean? Was she being sarcastic?

And so, the whole merry dance of trying to unpick what someone means on an email versus in the flesh unfolds.

Sometimes we need to see the human person in front of us and assess that they are not a dinosaur or a wild boar sent to kill us. We need to see their body language and the way they say their feedback to us and then respond with questions, and in this context we can get any misunderstandings cleared up more readily. I am not arguing that we do everything face to face as this would be unrealistic, but I often feel that work feedback needs to be in person or you are effectively dropping a bad-vibes bomb into someone's lap and letting it slowly release toxic ruminations until you see them again and they get a chance (if they're confident enough) to ask you for more detail on what you've said.

If you get an email from a colleague and immediately feel yourself ruminating too much over the content and perhaps thinking that they mean something bad/hate you/want to sack you immediately then I give you this simple advice:

- Take a deep breath.
- Make yourself a cup of tea.
- Sit down.
- Write down on a piece of paper what you want to get across to this person in two or three bullet points.
- Pick up the phone and call them.

Or if you can't call them, ask to speak to them in person when you're next in the office. Use old-style analogue, bad-boy face-to-face conversation. You'll be amazed at how much clearer and less ambiguous it can be and how much relief you'll feel compared with thinking too hard about what someone might have meant in a piece of online communication.

It's hard to pretend we are robots

When you are young and full of beans then you might have the energy to compete with robots out there and reply to messages within three seconds and check all your communication platforms over and over until you go to bed. You may be fine to respond to a message so fast that you are tapping a reply while the person is finishing off their message to you.

You may get a buzz out of it.

The thing I've observed, though, is that it will probably give you a twitch and make you feel sick too. It will make you feel as if you've left the oven on. It's not just about age, it's more about our human, soft fleshy-ness.

You might have noticed that some of this 'your body is a machine' language creeps into our work vernacular. We ask people if they 'have capacity' instead of saying, 'Hey, do you have a few minutes to look at this thing and add your comments?'

We say we're 'drained' (like batteries). We increasingly expect to keep up with the speed of technology but forget that our bodies (especially as we age) are floppy and need to lie down sometimes and our brains can't focus when there are 400 tabs always open.

Then we also have these monitors that we wear on our bodies and perhaps that gives us the idea that we are machines and if we track everything we will live forever (and work forever).

Sometimes when we're pinging messages back and forth we can forget that there are people involved. So it becomes a way to just tap our thoughts into or to issue commands. We don't have to see the other person or their expression when they receive that message. On Slack, at its worse, it can feel that you're simply liking stuff and doing thumbs up so you can demonstrate that you are involved. There are days when it feels as if replying to content from other people is all you do and there isn't any time set aside to get work done.

'I got four hours' sleep,' an ex-colleague of mine said to me glancing at his techno-watch-gizmo-Google thing (can't remember the brand), 'This thing is brill because it breaks it all down. How much REM, how much lighter sleep, how long it took.'

'But does it make you feel better having all that information? I mean, you still didn't sleep?'

He looked at me as if I was mad. I have noticed this a lot with people who measure everything. They don't understand the people who don't. If you are someone who loves apps to measure all your bodily functions, then that's fine but just also trust your gut. If you need to lie down, do it.

The more we behave like robots, the more people will treat us as such. Tap into your humanity. Do things that only humans can do. Empathise. Use your intuition. Speak. Resist the urge to type to the person sitting next to you. Resist the urge to wear headphones all day in the office. Resist.

How we need to remember our physical bodies and pay respect to them

Newsflash! We get periods. We have hormones that can get in the way of how we're performing. We have babies. We go through the menopause. And let's just park the idea of male versus female; it's not natural to:

- get off a flight and present to an entire team without getting any rest first
- sit at a laptop for eight hours straight and eat your lunch at your desk, munching your sandwich so quickly that you can't even remember what you're eating and must read the description on the front of the packet
- wake up every morning feeling more tired than when you went to bed
- have an upset tummy every day
- have headaches all the time
- look at beds when you walk past bed shops and get an overriding desire to just get into the bed and curl up and go to sleep
- cry on planes (not just when watching films) because you can't face getting off at the other end because you have four days straight of work with no break
- do a debrief after you've just spent six hours moderating groups and your throat hurts.

And *it is normal* to get a goddamn cold, to stop, to rest, to have a break, to ring a friend, to stay at home because you are menopausal and can't cope, to feel hormonal and less able to navigate tricky situations at work, to get a backache and lie down on the floor to stretch your back, to have a nice lunch that you can taste and remember, to have a healthy body, to stretch, to step outside and feel sunshine on your face for a bit.

We need to take care of our bodies as nobody else is going to do that job

More recently, I started to think about the idea of being an athlete in more detail and I realised that if you define it in the right way, maybe it's not so bad. So, as you age you tend to feel less robust, you get more tired, you feel more anxious (maybe), you may be getting less sleep and suffering from either child-related or hormone-related sleep disorders, and the thing is, if you want to work and do good work then you must respect your health and you must take it seriously. It may sound creepy that a healthier you is a more productive you – like an advert for supplements targeting superwomen back in the 1980s – but the truth is it's useful to think about how you treat your body and how you feel at work and do the best you can to eliminate the stuff that makes work even more challenging.

For me, those things are:

- drink
- drugs
- no sleep (this is out of my control though as I have small kids)
- no breaks
- no exercise
- scrolling on my phone too much
- being cooped up inside for too long
- nothing to look forward to except for more work and deadlines for the foreseeable future…

So, if those things are similar for you and they make you feel shitty at work and anxious (and this is not about working non-stop for 36 hours) then experiment with cutting some of them out.

Some self-care tips for when you're feeling fragile and working hard

- Take a walk, ideally somewhere where you can see the sky. Focus on looking upwards and leave your phone in your pocket. Look at the clouds and focus on the different shapes you can see (this really helps bring you into the moment and be present rather than thinking about what you still have to do).
- Watch something incredibly silly on TV. For me, watching half an hour of a reality TV show like *Below Deck* really helps me switch off. If I'm having a stressful day, I will watch this at lunchtime and it requires no thinking and no analysis. It is as if I've switched my brain off completely.
- Make a stew. On the days that I work from home I find something really comforting about making a stew. I am not talking Nigella-style here. I am talking ripping open a packet that you stir into some chopped up vegetables and then flinging a packet of sausages in there and putting it in the oven. There is something very therapeutic and grounding about cooking when you're frazzled (again, it encourages you to be in the moment and not project into the future or worry about the past).
- Phone a friend – all too often we feel that we haven't got time to chat to a friend and we use texts instead. Sometimes when you're feeling preoccupied by work, a chat with a friend is the thing you need to bring things into perspective. You can vent a bit and rant and then let it go again. I often

find a ten-minute chat with someone who really gets you is more therapeutic than an Epsom salts bath and a face mask (though they also work too especially if you listen to a podcast at the same time).

- Move your body – any kind of exercise helps when we're stressed or thinking a lot about work. Exercise not only produces endorphins – the feel-good hormones – but also takes us out of our own heads for a while. I try and do a short burst of exercise on the mornings that I'm working because it helps clear my head when I've woken up feeling anxious because I know I've got a lot on.

Also, a note on working in the evenings. Sometimes (especially as a working mum) you can get into the habit of putting the kids to bed and picking work up again. A bit of this now and then is okay but remember that you need time to rest and switch off. Working just before you go to bed is likely to keep you awake at night because your brain will still be fizzing from all the stuff you've been working on. You might start getting into an unhealthy pattern of working until really late and this isn't helpful for you or your colleagues (who might then get emails late at night that set them on edge and make them think that working late is what's required when really it's just you trying to squeeze more work in).

Remember that you can only really focus on work for a short amount of time and then you need to rest. You won't be doing your best work if you keep at it for ages, and you're more likely to make mistakes too.

A note on sleep deprivation and work

I'll talk about parenting and work and that specific beast later in this book but let's be honest, when you are in the early stages of parenting you don't sleep. In fact, you don't sleep when they're teenagers either apparently (this is what I hear from friends because you're worried about where they are at night. For a long time the fact that I was never getting enough sleep and yet trying to be productive at work stressed me out. I would be woken in the night by one of my kids and would then be unable to sleep because I'd be so worried about the impact of no sleep on my day. Or I'd be (and am now) woken at 5 and then worry about how crap I'll be at work all day.

The thing is this. Sleep deprivation is hell. It is bad. It *is* bad. It impacts on your mood and your immune system and if you dare Google it, it will reveal that you can die from it (long term).

It impacts on your ability to make decisions, to remember things, to pay attention. It also affects your auditory and visual-spatial attention and impacts on how fast you can react to things.[10]

Sleep deprivation is especially acute when you have children and yet employers don't seem to address this fact when parents return to work after their parental leave. It means that many parents are impaired but are too frightened to admit that this is happening. In all honesty employers *should* consider moving to a more flexible working pattern for new parents (it is to be hoped that more sleep comes as your children get older) so that they're not trapped in offices for long hours and barely functioning. There should be sleep pods provided so they can take a nap. It is not a luxury to sleep, it is a necessity, and while everyone knows that new parents don't sleep, there is little done in terms of thinking about how heavily this impacts on their relationship with work. Sleep deprivation also happens at other times of life like menopause or times of the month or because you're stressed, and – here's the secret – I am not going to say that you can go without sleep for a long time and be okay *but* I will say that if you're stuck in a bout of no sleep or poor sleep, you will survive. Just make sure that you are resting your body whenever you get the opportunity.

---

10 www.ncbi.nlm.nih.gov/pmc/articles/PMC2656292

If you're working from home then this means occasionally lying on the floor and stretching out (this is something you should do anyway). It also means doing the odd meditation session now and then to switch off your brain. Or for me it means watching *Below Deck* on Netflix while eating my lunch because it makes me relax and switch off. Ultimately, you can still be clever and say clever things and be tired. You will survive. I think looking back I've had no sleep, or not a proper night of sleep, for about seven years now. I am not saying it's ideal, but I am okay. I have to go to bed early and I can't really deal with work socials because I yawn non-stop but I will survive... *as will you.*

Avoid your phone first thing

Recently, I have been trialling something where I don't pick up my phone first thing in the morning. This was after talking to a male colleague who said that getting stuck into his phone first thing didn't help. So now I wake up (usually to the dulcet tones of my toddler screaming 'Mum' loudly and I stumble into her room to retrieve her before she wakes my older daughter up). I try hard not to look at my phone until I'm downstairs and have had a coffee.

'The thing is, you can often read something that puts you in a bad mood and then your day has got off to a shit start,' a colleague said.

I struggle but this is something I believe to be true. I also drink water. I avoid booze if I'm having an intense period at work or starting a new job as I know I will be anxious and don't need to pile more anxiety onto the whole thing.

I also check in on my smell. I know the smell is a good gauge of how stressed I am. I will address work and anxiety later but the smell is a start. Oh, and remembering that the adage, 'I'll sleep when I'm dead' is only said by losers, if it's applied to overwork, pushing your body to the brink and sacrificing your health.

Let's move away from the idea that our bodies are machines. Let's remember that we are human. As we age this becomes even more clear because your body starts talking to you and telling you that it doesn't like what you're doing. Find the things that make you feel healthy but don't do this for the sake of being productive. Do this because you want to feel good and live longer.

I spoke to Eleanor Noon who is the Founder and Editor in Chief of Noon, a platform to empower women in midlife, and who was Editorial Director at *The Sunday Times*. She shared her experiences of the old world of work and how self-care was pretty much absent.

> When I was at *The Sunday Times*, every Friday we started work at 9 a.m., or before, and didn't finish until 2 a.m. because of the print deadlines. I worked those hours through both of my pregnancies, and the next job I had, as Focus Editor, in charge of the big breaking stories of the week, came with an office equipped with a camp bed. My predecessor often slept there on Friday nights! The long hours' culture was just part of life on a newspaper.

In some ways, she feels that technology is a liberating force but has fostered a different kind of omnipresent work culture.

> I suppose in some ways technology has freed us from that kind of physical presentism but now we are all supposed to be available 24/7. At least in the old days once you had left, you had left. I am currently setting up a new business and with the pandemic and a mobile phone connected to email and social media, the boundary between work and non-work seems to have become non-existent – to the point that for my own mental health I now leave my phone downstairs in the kitchen when I come up to bed, and my husband insists

that it gets turned off. Otherwise you never switch off – and that is the danger. There is no point in sitting on a beautiful beach on a sunny day if your head is in your email – you might as well be at a desk in front of a computer. That kind of fractured presence is the new workaholism – that busyness can be addictive and needs to be kept firmly under control.

I asked Eleanor whether she felt that mental and physical health was more of a priority now at work and she warns about a culture that looks as if it's being designed for our benefit but is more about keeping us tied into work for more hours (i.e. encouraging people not to leave their workplaces by situating everything they need within one office complex).

I think companies are more sympathetic about mental health issues now, but there is still massive shame from those who are suffering from it; much easier to admit to a broken leg than a broken mind. However, the constantly on, never off work culture is contributing to a new kind of always-on burnout which can be more insidious. And the idea that we should sacrifice everything on the altar of a job, or a company, which, whatever they may claim, never loves us back is wrong. I am worried about some of the emergent corporate cultures which promise total wrap-around care but are really just trying to extend the hours worked.

Ultimately, we must be the guardians of our own health and retain a perspective in terms of what's important and what isn't. Our bosses won't always be looking out for us:

As my mum always used to say: the graveyards are full of indispensable chief executive officers, politicians, editors and so on – the only people we are really indispensable to are our families. To a company, you are always just a number on a spread sheet in the end.

She adds that the conversations around the menopause have opened up but pushes back against too much emphasis being put on women's physical make-up:

> There is definitely more of a conversation, but I don't know how helpful it always is – I didn't want to be defined by my biology as a younger woman and I certainly don't want to be now. But it is important that the 25 per cent of women who have real problems with the menopause are looked after appropriately and society is more aware of the kind of issues they face.

Eleanor's tips for self-care are also around being more mindful about phone use and not letting technology destroy any boundary between work and home.

> Learn how to say no. Switch off your mobile phone or leave it downstairs when you go to bed. Build in times when you are not going to go near your phone and stick to them, really clear your mind and be present where you are. Do something you love; though in some ways being gripped by purposeful work makes it even hard to turn off the laptop and stop working, because it is your passion too! However, that is a good problem to have.

As we age, we need to protect our health and cut ourselves some slack. In fact, at any age this is true. There is nothing brave about ignoring symptoms that you're about to burn out. And there is nothing admirable about going into work with flu and passing it on to all your colleagues.

Your body needs rest. This is not just so you can 'perform more effectively' or 'be more productive'. Remember, you are a marvellous, curious, exciting creature with blood, veins, moods and a breathtaking imagination. You could never be a machine.

Who would even want to be one anyway?

The 'Write That Shit Out'/Gratitude Exercise
That Helps You Focus and Get Stuff Done

I am prone, like many women, to rumination. As I hit my mid-forties this tendency seemed to get worse or perhaps I just paid more attention to it because I noticed other friends also admitted they did a lot of ruminating.

Some ruminating is helpful. The kind that helps you arrive at a decision or solve a problem.

Some ruminating is not helpful because it's just your brain churning around and around on one message and you don't move any closer to a resolution; instead, it just keeps going. This is often what happens in the middle of the night, if you wake up suddenly, or can happen if you've had a particularly busy day at work and you are finding it hard to switch off.

There is one thing that has really helped me quiet this ruminating and has helped me focus on what I need to do. I find it particularly useful in the morning, usually when I've just got up and have my first cup of coffee. It's not just something I invented. It's an actual thing and is called 'morning journaling'. I use it to stop the ruminating because I tend to wake up with a lot of stuff on my mind and worries for the day ahead. It can also be used in lots of other ways too. So, you can write down:

- three things you feel grateful about
- the thing you need to tackle that day that you can't ignore (i.e. the thing you've been putting off)

- what your big dream is – not just for today but overall. This helps you keep a sense of perspective and makes you feel excited. It can be a massive dream like 'I want to be a bestselling author' – it should be something big ideally.

Then also just do a literal brain dump – which is every thought that is floating about in your head. Once it's down then you'll feel a sense of relief.

Here's a typical brain dump that I'd write down first thing:

I need to learn how to create a code on the admin system but have no idea how to do it and when I tried to do it last time, it went wrong, even though I sat next to my colleague and she talked me through the steps, one at a time. If I can't create that code then who else is going to do it? Is there anyone else who can do it? I can't do it because I have no idea how to do it and when I tried it last time it went wrong, even though I sat next to my colleague and she talked me through the steps, one at a time.

And I keep writing. Eventually I might write something like: *'Find colleague who knows how to create code and ask them if they can do it, then double-check this time that it is working, also write down everything she does so I can do it myself next time.'*

Then my brain starts to stop fizzing. Because that's how it feels when you're ruminating and ruminating – it's like an unpleasant fizz that gets in the way of enjoying time with your family or watching TV or just letting go and relaxing. Write it out of your system. It will give you peace. It will help you let go. It works.

CHAPTER FOUR

Work Anxiety and How to Navigate a Way Through

Work anxiety is very common and you're not the only one feeling it

Everyone I have ever worked with has been anxious at work at some time. If they say this isn't true then they're lying. We all get butterflies or feel a bit sick or worry that something will go wrong and we are built to be this way. If we were cavewomen then this anxiety would have saved us from being eaten by bears (we would have run into a cave to hide) but now the problem is that we often have the same physical symptoms firing up when we're at work (and it's not actually a life or death situation).

In fact, a 2020 survey by Perk box revealed that 79 per cent of British adults had experienced work-related stress. Fifty-five per cent percent had experienced anxiety because of this stress. The most anxiety-inducing thing? 'Work-related office politics' apparently, with long working hours given as the seventh highest cause of stress. And interestingly, older people – those aged 45–54 – were most likely to get stressed by 'work-related office politics'.[11]

Interestingly, these 'work-related office politics' may be things that actually exist (i.e. real people doing stupid things that annoy us and getting up in our grills with their competitive vibes) but

11 www.perkbox.com/uk/resources/library/2020-workplace-stress-survey

I imagine that some of this politics is stuff that's tied up with our own self-image and negative self-talk (i.e. I'm older, I'm less relevant, others are better than me, and so on).

When I tried to come up with a title for this chapter, I wanted to come up with a word that combined work and anxiety. The best I could come up with was 'wanxiety' which doesn't sound great (sounds as if you are anxious because you're masturbating too much), but there is a very particular kind of anxiety that is related to work and can be more challenging and persistent than other types of anxiety. First off, we are often in a state of stress at work. It is impossible to avoid stress because there are deadlines, navigating different personalities, managing expectations, setting boundaries (or failing to), and so it's normal to feel anxious on a regular basis. Sometimes it might present itself first thing in the morning when you wake up and think of all the stuff you must do that day. Other times it might come in the middle of the day as a tidal wave of overwhelm. Then it can also crop up at night when you're in bed and suddenly sit up and remember that you haven't answered one of the emails that you thought you had and need to do it immediately.

I am often suspicious of people who don't get anxious at work.

Anxiety is a ball ache whichever way you look at it but it seems to increase incrementally when we age. There are some other equations it's worth thinking about too:

Age + new job + global pandemic that might return perhaps + young children + fear that everyone else is more qualified = a massive shit storm of anxiety.

What happens when I get anxious?

So first up I notice the physical symptoms. These are always the same. A churning stomach. Then a headache.

Then the next thing is the negative voice that starts telling me in no uncertain terms that something catastrophic is about to happen – either that I've made a massive mistake at work or I'm about to screw something up.

Then my brain looks for evidence – anything it can find from the past in terms of examples where I have screwed up or embarrassed myself in a meeting (and the stupid thing is there haven't been many examples but my brain will work super hard to find them anyway).

One of the things I've noticed is that my anxiety is often worse first thing in the morning. I've talked about the importance of morning routines and how they help to set the day, and it's taken me a while to learn this.

When my first daughter was born, I used to wake up each morning in those newborn days with a feeling of overarching dread. Then it hit again when I had my second daughter. And it returned more recently when I started a new job. The thing is that when your anxiety is really bad it's hard to use any tools or strategies to make yourself feel better because you simply feel trapped. One useful thing I've started to do when I wake up with this dread anxiety is something I've learned from Mel Robbins' *The High 5 Habit, Take Control of Your Life with one Simple Habit*. She recommends a simple technique where you put your hand on your heart and say the words, 'I am okay, I am safe, I am loved.' At first I thought this idea was *way* too cheesy but if you take a deep breath and try it when you're feeling seriously anxious you'll find it helps. It stops some of the catastrophising, drags you back into the moment and is almost like giving yourself a hug. The other thing to remind yourself is that anxiety is a feeling and it will pass. It always does. In the same book, Robbins also advises that you give yourself a 'high five' in the mirror each morning to switch off your negative thinking and set you on the right path for the day. I also thought this sounded silly but I tried it and it worked, so it's another tool to have in your repertoire during anxious times.

Those moments when you're trapped inside the physical and emotional symptoms of anxiety are troubling because they also impact on your work performance. You might feel less able to communicate clearly – so you may come across as being defensive or overly emotional. You are in fact more likely to make mistakes which then feed back into your anxiety and the story you're telling yourself about how you're about to fuck everything up.

So, this diagram illustrates the kind of pattern you end up with:

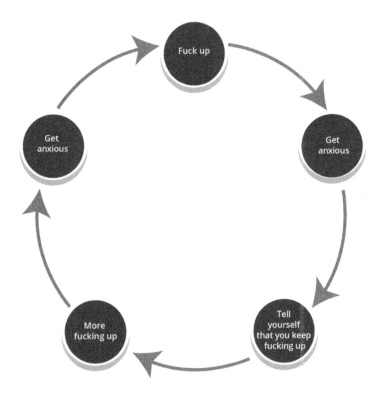

I call this the *cycle of work anxiety fuckery*. It's total *wanxiety* (don't know if that term will take off but hey ho).

It's basically no fun and once you're in the thick of it, it's hard to break out.

There is also another misconception about work-related anxiety and that is you're the *only* one going through it. I've met enough brilliant women (and men too) to know that just about everyone gets it. The woman in the corner who is looking very cool and saying the clever things that everyone is nodding their head to – she suffers with it.

The young woman who has just presented a game-changing social media strategy to a room full of ten people and hasn't broken into a sweat – she has it too. And it manifests itself in different ways. Some women become very productive and obsessed by busyness. Others enter a slump and find it hard to get anything done at all.

Here's Lena Dunham talking about her mental health in May 2016:

> I've always been anxious, but I haven't been the kind of anxious that makes you run ten miles a day and make a lot of calls on your Blackberry. I'm the kind of anxious that makes you be like, 'I'm not going to be able to come out tonight, tomorrow night or maybe for the next 67 nights.[12]

And US actress Kerry Washington, discussing how important it is to talk about our mental health and treat it seriously:

> I think it's really important to take the stigma away from mental health… My brain and my heart are important to me. I don't know why I wouldn't seek help to have those things be as healthy as my teeth. I go to the dentist. So why wouldn't I go to a shrink?

---

12 www.thecut.com/2020/09/25-famous-women-on-dealing-with-anxiety-and-depression.html

The woman in her sixties who has her own business and has written three acclaimed books and is doing a TED talk all about empowered women in their sixties – well, she has it too. And even that guy who is acting all manly and punching the air and is heading up his own fancy app that delivers dog food on demand – he has it.

So many people experience anxiety, but some have found ways to get around it and ways to continue being productive. They find strategies and tools to turn things around. (But there are debilitating levels of anxiety and I've had these too. These are when you feel as if you can't do anything and can't even get out of bed. In this situation, you need to seek professional help and contact your GP.)

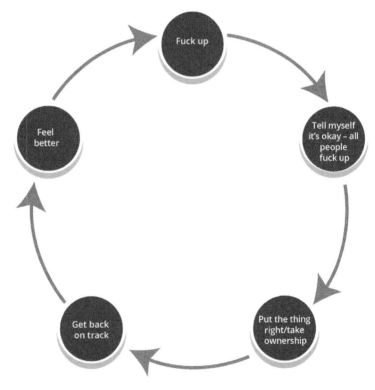

These tools are not revolutionary – and like the self-care that we talked about in the previous chapter, it's all about spotting when anxiety is about to strike and then coming in with a different thought process. For me it's represented as this:

So, once you realise that it's normal to make mistakes at work, and when something goes wrong, acknowledge it is a mistake, put it right and move on, then you've broken out of the cycle. Importantly, don't let it define your work personality and don't keep telling people about the mistakes you've made.

Anxiety related to being in your forties and older

I have now got a new anxiety to add to my list of anxieties and it is this: I am often the oldest person in the office. While I have written an entire book about how to age and not feel shit, I still have a little voice in my head that tells me I am not good enough because I am the oldest person in the office. I currently work in social media and on bad days I have a recurring voice which says stuff like, *What a stupid old witch you are! How can you claim to be good at social media when you don't even know what's in the charts anymore? Or that there aren't any charts nowadays? You have to Google stuff after each meeting!*

The thing is, I am the oldest person in the office. I must remind myself that there is nothing I can do about this fact. The age thing is just one aspect of who I am. It is not just a number because I think if we say that then we are basically just shoving our age under the carpet. I am 48 and have lived through some pretty lame chart music and some dreadful fashion trends, and survived.

I haven't yet touched on the symptoms of perimenopause or menopause which are still rarely discussed in the world of work. Anxiety and feelings of depression and low mood are very common as the body starts to prepare for the menopause. It can make even simple work tasks and interactions feel challenging and it can also feel very isolating because women don't want to admit that they're going through these hormonal changes (and may not even be aware that they are due to the perimenopause or menopause because we don't talk enough about these changes and how common they are).

If you are having age-related anxiety and the voice in your head is making you feel bad, just write down a list of the things that you bring to your role. Many of these things have been learned over time. You have done them again and again.

Here is my list. These are the things I tell myself when I am going through age-related anxiety. You can create your own list – and remember, you don't need to show it to anyone (but you can if you want to, of course).

- I am creative.
- I am great at coming up with ideas.
- I am empathetic.
- I make mistakes but when I make them, I learn from them.
- I am good at writing (you may disagree with this but I hope not if you've read this far).
- I use humour to keep teams motivated and to lighten the mood.
- I work quickly and get tasks done easily.
- I have faced challenges in the past and have managed to navigate a way through them.
- I have worked with a lot of difficult and downright fucking annoying people and have still managed to produce good work (and not killed anyone in the process).
- It's okay if people think I'm old. I can live with that.

Another strategy is to keep emails that people have sent you or WhatsApp messages that have praise and positive things in them. All too often we have a tendency to dwell on the negative things and this is another way of helping reprogramme your neural pathways so you can think about the times when you have done a good presentation or written a great piece of copy or helped on a project that you thought would be a downright disaster. You'll be amazed when you start thinking about how much you've achieved (you might want to take Robbins' advice and give yourself a 'high five', or if that's too effusive for you then why not just raise one eyebrow in the mirror?).

Keep your own list of positive things and praise near you always. Or just write down quotes when they say things to your face. Each time the negative voice starts, come up with a counter argument. Ping an elastic band on your wrist to stop yourself going down that dark hole that leads to nowhere (the one that tells you that your work life/your entire life is over and it's all downhill from here on in).

Remember that we all tend to have a negative bias – this means we are more likely to remember negative stimuli or things that happen to us and dwell on these events. It is important to keep pushing back against this and reminding yourself of the positive things you've achieved.

Anxiety and returning from maternity leave

When I came back from maternity leave, a restructure had happened in my company and the people I'd hired were now my bosses. I felt furious but I also felt tremendously insecure and spent my time apologising and shouting in equal measure (the shouting usually happened in front of friends and family, not in front of work colleagues). The only thing that got me through was two friends at work who believed in me and kept being supportive, and writing a book about the whole thing (it was fiction but contained a couple of elements that were true to life). This emotional support – the writing and the friends – helped me navigate one of the most unpleasant work experiences of my life.

Anxiety when you return from maternity leave is common. It's often hard to navigate as you've been out of the office loop for a while, people have been promoted and hired in your absence and the systems and procedures in place might have changed too. My advice here is simple – be patient with yourself. The things that you notice that you're not doing well are probably not being noticed by others. Don't flag up your deficiencies. Keep a positive mindset and say you can do something and then find someone who can help you learn how to do it. Use Google if desperate. I use Google all the time. This is a time when you'll need a robust tool kit so make a list of the things that help you feel less anxious and be sure to include a couple of these each week (ideally one every day, such as a hot bath, a short meditation or a chat with a friend). Write your fears on paper. If nothing else, you can use them to fuel a poem or a novel. Ask for training if you feel severely on the back foot.

Remember that employing a mother is not something you should feel grateful to your employer for. You have a million transferable skills. Also invest in a white shirt (but you don't need to wear a boring grey blazer and can afford to wear colour. Don't conform to the stereotypes of women at work – unless you love grey blazers that is). There is nothing that makes you look more together than a white shirt (even if it has avocado smashed all over the collar from feeding your baby that morning).

Ditch the self-deprecation vibes

This diagram effectively shows how the more self-deprecating you are as a woman, the more people will like you. It is a highly effective strategy but it is possible to be successful at work without everyone liking you (they could instead respect you).

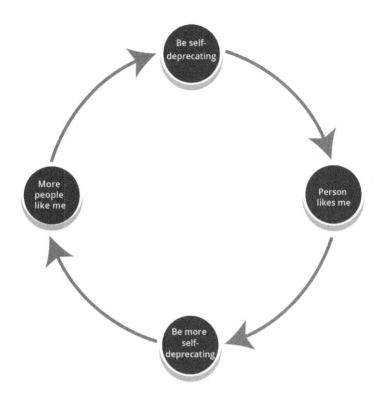

It helps make us more relatable. When women don't do this, they are perceived as cold or a bit standoffish. This comes back to our social conditioning and the fact that as women we are taught to always be likeable and agreeable, no matter how we feel inside. So, say you compliment me on my dress and state, 'Ooh that colour really suits you. It makes your skin really glow.' What do you want me to say back? Well, one answer (and the one I would have commonly given) would have been, 'This old dishcloth? I salvaged it from a skip on my run this morning. It stinks!' That way I would have immediately felt that I was making myself relatable and the colleague would be more likely to give me approval.

But what if you just accepted the compliment? And when someone compliments you on a job well done, don't say, 'Well, I'm useless at strategic thinking so this was the next best thing.' Instead, say, 'Thanks. I worked hard. I'm glad you're happy with it. I think it's great.'

Stop making yourself small. Stop apologising and this too will feed into your thought patterns and help to convince you that you are doing stuff that deserves praise.

NB: If you've made a massive mistake then it's not great to hide it – for example, if you've disconnected the entire company server and put it in your trash then you need to fess up. Take ownership but then apologise and move on, and don't see it as a sign that you're useless at everything.

The fighting anxiety in the toilet technique

Later, in the book, I talk about crying in the toilet as I seriously believe it's a valid way of letting go of tension at work. It can also work when you're feeling anxious. So, if you're in a state of high anxiety and you are in the office and feeling those familiar sensations – maybe rapid heartbeat, stomach flutterings, headache – here are some easy things to do to make yourself feel better in the moment:

- Get yourself to the toilet, go into a cubicle and if you're in the cubicle on your own do a big sigh.
- Next do some breathing techniques to steady yourself – breathe in for four and out for five, in for four and out for five.
- Or use a breathing app and try one of their recommended techniques. Breathing is the first step to feeling better.

- While in the cubicle, sing a little song to yourself about your anxiety – there is a great book called *The Worry Trick: How Your Brain Tricks You Into Expecting the Worst and What You Can Do About It,* which outlines why this works. I like to sit on the toilet seat and I sing a song that goes:

  I'm feeling shit and my heart is pounding.
  So, crap and I can't bear it.
  Why am I feeling like this? Why?
  Maybe it's because I had no sleep and there's a meeting starting in ten and I have no idea what it's about.

This song isn't going to top the charts or win any Brit Awards. The technique is more about putting distance between yourself and your thoughts so you can see the thoughts for what they are – thoughts, not real life.

I spoke to Kim Palmer, founder of the hypnotherapy app *Clementine*, about her history of suffering with anxiety. Her experiences working in the corporate world, earlier in her career helped her come up with the idea for the app.

> At the time, I didn't know I had anxiety. I just thought it was normal to be on the edge all the time, to feel sick in my stomach all the time, to be tired all the time and have headaches and to constantly doubt myself. I wrapped up a lot of my self-worth in work and being 'great at everything' which now I look back was incredibly unhealthy. I was a perfectionist, cared too much, couldn't let work go at the end of the evening or at the end of the week, I carried work in my head 24/7.

For Kim, becoming pregnant was the catalyst for things to change after negating her true feelings for so long. Suddenly, everything bubbled to the surface in a frightening and disorientating way:

> Looking back, it's easy to see that I was about to burst. It took becoming pregnant for my anxiety to tip over the edge. I made a conscious decision to almost forget that I was pregnant and became even more obsessed with the idea that I needed to secure a promotion before I had my first baby. So I took on more responsibility, worked harder and didn't look after myself mentally, which lead to me experiencing my first panic attack at work. It was so traumatic, because I felt like I had lost my status as 'having it all together'. It was embarrassing and then I just started to hide and that's when my anxiety and panic attacks took over and I lost my confidence and my voice for quite some time. Back then no one talked about anxiety. I wouldn't have had the foggiest idea what it even was. It just wasn't spoken about.

Kim found there were practical things that helped her navigate her way through anxiety but first off it was important for her to acknowledge that anxiety wasn't going to go away. It would always be present in some form. Kim elaborates:

> First things first, I try to ditch all the pressure to 'ditch anxiety'. It's a bit like the idea of striving for balance, striving for perfection. I have now realised that even just the idea that I need to fix something makes things worse for me. So rather than ditching anxiety, I see it as my friend. Sounds strange though. It's just part of me and when I feel it then I know that something about my life needs a bit of retuning. But before any retuning starts, I sit with the anxiety. I find that sitting with the feelings is so helpful because you can learn more about why you feel like that in the first place. And, weirdly,

that when you sit in the feelings and don't try to push and fix, they pass through quicker.

Whereas before Kim would have tried to cover up her real feelings, she is now more aware of what's going on and can ask herself questions on what's setting these feelings in motion in the first place, then take the steps she needs to work on these:

> I will also ask myself questions when I'm feeling anxious: what could it be that's going on right now that might be triggering these feelings? Home, work, kids, sleep, exercise, money? Sometimes I need to write this all out on paper too, to help me make sense of what I'm feeling. Then I hatch a plan to shift something that might be triggering me, or reset a boundary. Actually, often my anxiety comes on because I have crossed too many of my own boundaries.

For people living with anxiety there are specific times of the day when it can flare up. So for me, morning has always been a tough time to navigate. Recognising the routines that work for you and help you feel calmer and more together are key. For Kim, mornings and evenings are important in shaping the way she is going to feel so she has developed a specific routine that is another resource in her toolbox:

> I have a very structured morning and evening routine that includes stuff that fills me with joy and helps me to ground myself. So, in the morning there are three things I will always protect like gold – sitting down and eating breakfast with my family. Yes, it's chaos, but I love the time to connect and not rush. The next is my morning walk. Sometimes I will listen to a *Clementine* 'visualise your day' session and sometimes I will not listen to anything. Then just before I start work, I make

myself a nice coffee. I only have one a day as I know more than that makes me feel anxious, so it's lovely to savour every last sip. For the evenings, I go to bed early around 9.30/10 p.m., read a book or magazine (always the physical) do a two- to five-minute massage in bed and then spray my sleep pillow mist. Lights out.

As Kim suggests, creating a strategy around mornings can be incredibly helpful because it gives us a set of things we do each day and hopefully sets us up on the right path. Here's my own example:

Anniki's Morning Routine That Really Works

I love reading about the morning routines of famous, successful people but often find that they're completely unrealistic unless you have a live-in nanny and personal trainer and someone who goes to the shops and makes sure you have granola and hemp milk and oranges so you can have a super healthy breakfast. There is, however, one thing I really agree with. A good morning routine will set you up for a good day.

I have small children so mornings are often not very calming but nonetheless I have found a few things massively helpful. They are small things but make a huge difference to the way I start the day. One of them is the journaling which I've outlined above. There are also a few other things I do:

- Exercise for half an hour: I subscribe to an online exercise platform and do 30 minutes every other day. The kids watch TV while I do this because they get up so early that we usually have two hours before I can drop them off at school/childcare. I leave my exercise bra and jogging bottoms at the bottom of the bed and I literally put them on with my eyes shut. I never used to be an exercising person because I thought it was something only models and actresses did. I am now an exercising person. This short dose helps me shake off anxiety and gets the endorphins flowing about.
- Caffeine: I know it's a cliché but I can't function without two strong coffees. I make a pot when I get up and I drink

most of that pot (so they must be giant coffees). I know it's not particularly healthy but this is my vice. I might give this up when the children are older and stop waking up so early but for now it is a big part of my routine.

- Nice shower gel and a mantra: This sounds trite and ridiculous but I always buy shower gels and bath stuff that say 'calming' on them. I get in the shower and I put some of the 'calming' whatever it is on a flannel and then I put the flannel on my face. I breathe deeply and say an affirmation. I know you might laugh at this idea but it honestly works. I used to get in the shower and think about the people I hated at work or the terrible thing I'd been putting off, but instead I put the flannel on my face and say something like, 'I am getting more successful each day,' and maybe I'll make myself laugh but, more importantly, I won't already be stuck in the negative brain churn bollocks which is hard to snap out of once you're in it. If the flannel and mantra don't work then I will literally talk to myself and say something like, 'Anniki, can you just chill the fuck out and remember that X is annoying but they're also quite nice so don't be quite so judgemental, okay?'

- Some sort of breakfast: This doesn't have to be something totally unachievable and so could just be toast and a banana (my breakfast is strongly shaped by what the kids eat for breakfast).

- Lay your outfit out the night before: If you're going in to work then it's good to have your outfit planned. I also put the clothes out for my kids too, so I don't have to think about them either. I find the less thinking I need to do the better.

- A really good podcast on the way to work: This has become a big part of my routine. I love podcasts and find that the journey into the office is the perfect time to listen to them. My favourites feature Glennon Doyle, Elizabeth Day, Adam Buxton, Brene Brown, Oprah Winfrey. I've also found that I pull out titbits of these podcasts during the day as they often touch on emotional issues that come up in life and work. I might also listen to an empowering podcast that has some 90s hip hop in there.

Think about your own morning routine and the things that make you feel better equipped to deal with whatever work throws at you. It has taken me 48 years to realise that mornings shape the rest of the day and if you get up and think about how much your life sucks and how much you hate work then you won't be giving yourself the best start at all.

Finally, the one thing I've learnt about anxiety, and this is especially true as you get older, is you are hopefully better at recognising the signs and hopefully better at knowing what will make you feel better in that moment. So, if you are starting a new job or going through a period of intense activity at work and finding it hard, pull out all the stops to make yourself feel better.

Being Burnt Out Is Not Aspirational Either

I had never really heard of the term 'burnout' until quite recently. Then it seemed as if everyone was talking about it. Sure, I'd witnessed people at work *at the end of their tether*. I'd seen people being signed off for months at a time. I'd also seen people drinking too much alcohol or taking drugs to escape their overloaded work brains. These things were brushed under the carpet. In some professions, they still are. The language of work is still masculine – we are *nailing it, killing it, bossing it, owning it.* Those terms don't evoke a feeling of rest or harmony with the world around us. Instead, they make it feel as if each day must be lived at full throttle like a Pepsi Max ad where everyone bungee jumps out of aeroplanes while making the rock and roll signal with both hands.

Work was about survival of the fittest. The weak fell by the wayside. You were a gladiator in a gold, spiked chariot and you were tearing up your colleagues' vehicles left, right and centre. It was the Wolf of Wall Street. Or Bruce Willis in a tight, white vest when he had spray on hair blowing up buildings and not stopping until he'd blown the entire city up. It was a macho idea of work.

There is, however, still a romantic idea around working hard and making your life your work. A BBC article explains how the old 1980s workaholic ethic is still present but in a different guise:

New studies show that workers around the world are putting in an average of 9.2 hours of unpaid overtime per week – up from 7.3 hours just a year ago. Co-working spaces are filled with posters urging us to 'rise and grind' or 'hustle harder'. Billionaire tech entrepreneurs advocate sacrificing sleep so that people can 'change the world'. And since the pandemic hit, our work weeks have gotten longer; we send emails and Slack messages at midnight as boundaries between our personal and professional lives dissolve.[13]

The article also talks about how whereas before we might put Wall Street hedge fund managers on pedestals, now we idolise tech entrepreneurs who often advocate working long and unsustainable hours. The article quotes Anat Lechner, a clinical professor of management at New York University:

'The old distinction of day and night or, "Let's work until five o'clock and then go have drinks and go to sleep at 10" is for the 20th Century. The 21st Century is very different,' says Lechner. 'We live in a culture that is 24/7. Social media is 24/7, communication is 24/7, Amazon Prime is 24/7, everything is 24/7. We don't have those fixed boundaries.'

Let me describe how burnout can creep up on you. I experienced this myself very recently.

I had been in a new job for three months. My kids were about to start school and childcare again and I realised that my thinking was becoming increasingly squiffy. I was having trouble saying the right words. I was getting people's names wrong. I was making mistakes at work, more regularly than usual. Next, I was feeling drained of energy, suffering headaches, had a furry tongue and then I started feeling very pessimistic.

I'll never get on top of all the stuff I have to do.

---

13   www.bbc.com/worklife/article/20210507-why-we-glorify-the-cult-of-burnout-and-overwork

I'm rubbish.

I am possibly even dying right now.

These thoughts became more and more top of mind until one Saturday afternoon I asked my other half to drop me off at A&E. I am not the kind of person who goes to doctors regularly and the last time I'd been in A&E was when I'd suffered a miscarriage but I had reached a stage where I seriously believed I was dying. I kept thinking that nobody was taking me seriously. My head was throbbing. My mouth constantly dry. My heart racing and this was happening from the moment I woke up in the morning to when I went to bed.

'I can tell you're under a lot of stress,' the doctor said. 'You have high blood pressure that needs to be treated too.'

'I don't think I'm unnaturally stressed,' I said.

Surely rising at five each day, cleaning, looking after kids, working in a new job, surviving a pandemic, getting new uniform sorted, more cleaning, buying presents for a kid's party that weekend, wrapping them, being woken at five, trying to pull off an entirely new job in a new role at the same time, surely that was just normal stress? The problem is that when you're stressed every day, it quickly becomes normal. And perhaps you forget what relaxed feels like. Waiting to see the doctor (and it was a long wait of two hours) was the first time I'd sat down and done nothing in maybe eight years. I didn't go on my phone. I didn't try and pick up some random, suspect object from under the table, I didn't sort up socks into pairs or look for the gift voucher that I'd left in my bag but had mysteriously gone missing. Instead, I stared at a man wearing no pants who was eating a jumbo bag of Doritos.

This is what doing nothing feels like, I thought. *I can't do anything because I feel too tired and I'm in hospital.*

Luckily, I came out the other side of this episode. I was given beta blockers for a few months and started to feel more normal again. Many would simply keep on going until the symptoms became even more serious.

I spoke to Flic Taylor, a journalist and writer who has a podcast called 'Everyday Burnout Conversations', in which she talks to different guests each week about their experiences of extreme stress. She underwent a similar experience of burnout.

Flic says that initially she wasn't aware that anything was wrong with her:

> I kept blinders on to stop me from looking at my burnout for a good 18 months. I refused to believe I was burning out. I felt it would be 'weak' to admit I couldn't do everything. I would prioritise work and my family above myself and my health. When I was working a punishing schedule I found guilt creeping in, so I'd spend any spare time I had doing stuff for my family. I felt the only way to conquer burnout was to work extra hard and cross more things off my to-do list.

As we age this idea that we must keep going at the same speed as we did when we were younger can exacerbate this incessant need to keep busy – we feel as if we have a point to prove and can keep up with people who are younger than us. We may also be working to escape from other issues like the fact that hormonally we're feeling out of whack or that we're feeling insecure or worried about our relationship. Sometimes working and keeping going is a protection mechanism to numb ourselves from other challenges.

Flic believes that burnout is a very different experience from stress – stress is something we're likely to encounter each day while we're working but her experience felt much more extreme:

> Burnout is no buzzword to throw around casually. In May 2019, the World Health Organisation classified it as a medical condition. In Japan, they even use the word 'karoshi', meaning

death from work. The most common causes of karoshi are heart attacks or strokes due to stress and starvation. This is brutal.

Some of us might feel that this description is far-fetched but Flic got to a stage where she could no longer ignore her symptoms:

> When I sat slumped on my bathroom floor, alone, lost, desperate and burnt out, I started to question my life and worth in this world. That moment told me that burnout is life threatening and cannot be resolved with a cup of tea and a face pack.

Burnout is the state of being exhausted and depleted of your mental, physical and emotional strength because you have worked too hard, given too much of yourself away and have endured prolonged or repeated stress. Interestingly, studies[14] suggest it can also have long-term health impact on your brain function and so affect your reaction time and processing skills.

Therefore, the macho myth of work as an endurance, an action movie with heroes who never sleep or take a hot bath with essential oils, isn't helpful – to put it simply, longer term you won't be able to function at work and will end up making mistakes and misjudging things because your brain is malfunctioning.

Flic felt physically and emotionally depleted:

> I was exhausted and running on empty. Extreme fatigue manifested as brain fog, a feeling of emptiness, and bouts of insomnia. My self-care currency changed for the worse. I neglected my needs and pushed my joy aside. Sugar for the shock came from a packet of biscuits, while wine was my

14 www.thehrdirector.com/business-news/diversity-and-equality-inclu-sion/uk-heading-towards-burnout-breakpoint

nightly alcoholic anaesthetic. All the wrong things became my staple toolkit. I no longer felt effective in my purpose or confident in my performance. I lost touch with my identity. Denial led me to withdraw. It all just mounted into a huge big pile of apathy. I was crumbling, both physically and mentally. I crashed into a pool of tears and lethargy. My exhaustion exhibited physical symptoms, including chest pain, heart palpitations, shortness of breath, gastrointestinal pain and headaches. I started to overeat junk for comfort and to help my anxiety and depression.

Flic believes women in their forties are most at risk from suffering with burnout as they're in that rush hour of life where they're simultaneously trying to care for children, ageing parents and balancing careers at the same time. There is also the domestic load and the fact that during the pandemic women were not only working and caring for children but were also doing more work around the home. Flic adds:

A recent study carried out by Boston Consulting Group found that mothers in the UK are having to do an additional 31 hours' housework each week than they did before the lockdown – and an average of 12 more hours of household chores than fathers.

Eventually, Flic recognised what was happening to her and is now better equipped to take steps to avoid burnout. She explains:

If ignored, your body will sound alarm bells that escalate until you come to a screeching halt or crash. I burned out to the extent that I had to take a year off paid work to recover. Never did I think I had reached such an extreme point of burnout. Now I prioritise my rest and sleep, and I try to eat healthier and move daily. I started to put in boundaries with both my work and home life. I began to ask and accept help. In a nutshell, I try to align my home and working environment to my values – this felt so alien to me at first.

When I spoke to other women, it became clear that one of the benefits of being older is that we are better at recognising when we're heading towards burnout and better at resolving it ourselves (but it is a good idea to seek professional help if you're feeling unwell).

I can tell when I am hurtling towards a burnout and I usually take a step back, sleep, go for a walk and get some fresh air, and hope that I've stopped in time to stop the burnout.

It's important that I try and put things into perspective. And I try to take breaks.

The self-care strategies that I've talked about earlier can all help head off burnout. However, it is also paramount that you look at your job, the culture it promotes and whether the working practices are healthy or not. We all need to work for money but it is not sustainable to keep working at an inhuman pace and stay healthy, so if you can't see any possibility of change on the horizon then you need to start looking for a new job, if possible.

There are some company cultures where the Bruce Willis school of macho working bollocks still exists. This can make it hard to push back and create boundaries because everybody around you is burnt out and frazzled and so you feel guilty because everyone is overworked and suffering poor mental health. Senior managers often shape the working culture of a company so if they're coming into work when they're sick and staying late and sending emails at 11 at night or breaking down and having tantrums when small things go wrong, it's a sign that you need to find another job.

In my experience, these cultures never mend themselves and instead there will just be a high churn of people coming in and leaving again. Put yourself first and when you interview for a new job look around you and try and get a sense of whether overload is something that's championed or not. Your mental health will thank you later.

CHAPTER FIVE

The Benefits of Taking Things Slow

What comes to mind when you hear the word 'slow'?

This is what pops into mine:

- Ancient tortoises on their back legs eating cabbage.
- Annoying people in the queue paying with loose change in the supermarket.
- People who only get their Oyster card out when they're in front of the bus driver rather than having it ready when they rush on.

These aren't positive associations. I don't see slow working as being effective or beneficial in any way. Slow means I get less work done. Slow means I have to work for longer.

But I forget that slow working has its place too. It is better for my health. It helps me work more mindfully and avoid miscommunication and mistakes. It also helps me be creative (creativity doesn't like to be rushed – good ideas often spring into your head when you're doing nothing, like taking a shower or just staring into space).

I need to practise more of what the Dutch call 'niksen' which is basically the art of doing nothing and just staring for a while.

Busyness is seriously overrated.

There was a time (pre-pandemic) when busyness was a badge of honour. The busier you were, the more kudos you were given.

I have chatted earlier about an example of one of my bosses who swore she never got jetlag so could stand up and work for 48 hours straight. There was another woman called Rachel who my colleagues used to joke about because she moderated so many groups in a week that instead of sleeping she would just climb upright into a wardrobe in a hotel, close her eyes for ten minutes and then move on to moderating her next group. I don't know if Rachel is still going these days but I suspect she experienced some sort of breakdown because this kind of frenetic workload isn't sustainable. The crows will come home to roost. The physical side of never stopping puts our bodies under a huge amount of stress. It's also not great in terms of coming up with good quality ideas or feeling inspired. When you're rushing through work you're more likely to make mistakes, and you're less likely to come up with new ways of looking at a problem (when our bodies are in fight or flight mode then we are purely focused on survival rather than having a more curious/open mindset).

When was the last time you bunked off for a bit?

I'm not recommending that you bunk off work on a regular basis. However, in order to function well at work and to feel inspired, you do need to rest. So, slowing down is about working at a slower pace *and* about gifting some time to yourself.

When we're parenting and working it often feels that this 'me time' is non-existent. It is squashed into the commute to the office or the two minutes you sit on the toilet and practise your deep breathing. It is important that you have the occasional day that doesn't include children *or* work. If it can't be a full day then it needs to be half a day. If it can't be that then it needs to be a couple of hours.

When I was at school, we used to take in a permission slip signed by our parents that meant we could miss PE. I hated PE. I hated my legs (and we had to wear very short skirts) and I was ridiculously useless at sport. It is important that you too have one of these permission slips. This one is different. This one is about ring-fencing some time that is not work or child related (and also not about domestic admin or tidying either).

I am giving you a permission slip. I have signed it. I am giving it to you so you can be reminded that you can take a day off work. And in that day, you do not need to clean the orange scum between the tiles in the bathroom. You don't need to race to Tiger to buy birthday gifts for a kid's party coming up this weekend. You don't have to try and bury the cat poo that has surfaced again right next to the back door.

Here you go:

PERMISSION SLIP FOR…(print and fill in your name here)

This slip entitles the above recipient to ONE DAY/HALF A DAY/TWO HOURS OFF. This day should be spent doing nothing work related or family related. It should not be spent doing admin either or anything in the cleaning or tidying sphere. It should be spent either lying on the bed or having a bath and then watching reality TV. I am giving the recipient the order not to feel guilty at any stage for this complete state of inactivity. I am confident that it is necessary.

Yours sincerely
Anniki Sommerville

The pressure of running out of time gets more intense as we age

When we get older, there can be this sneaking suspicion that we're running out of time and this results in us feeling as if we must achieve everything at breakneck speed. There can also be a sense of comparing ourselves to younger colleagues (perhaps those without children) and feeling as if we're not keeping up because we're not putting in so many hours.

This speed thing – the idea that you must work hard each time that you are 'at work' – results in burnout. It's not pleasant and if you've been through it, you'll know that the tell-tale signs are things like crying more often than usual, trying to text your friend through the TV remote and forgetting your mother's maiden name when prompted by Barclays Bank. It is rapidly followed by screaming at the children because they don't like the katsu curry that you tried to make 'as a nice change' but tastes like wallpaper paste.

The point is you can't work all the time. You don't want to work all the time. What is that famous phrase? All work and no fun makes Jack a dull boy. Do you remember the scene when Jack Nicholson had typed that out on the typewriter in that classic horror film, *The Shining*? Well, what I'm saying is, we know how that film ended. We know that Jack Nicholson (sorry, spoiler alert, but it's a very old film so you must have seen it by now) ended up dead and his family almost murdered. He was suffering from more than just burnout but he missed the tell-tale signs that were telling him to *slow down*, to stop working (or writing in his case). Nobody could save him.

As I've already touched on, this speeding up has led us to believe that we need to communicate quickly too. So we speak less on the phone, text all the time, feel impatient when people don't get to the point quickly enough and are frustrated when we receive any email that is over four or five lines – *Christ! Do they really think I've got five minutes to read this shit?* (I also think there is a big difference reading mail on your phone where everything looks smaller and longer than it does on your laptop. I try now not to answer all my mails on my phone as I'm liable to misinterpret something important because my need for speed is even more pronounced when it comes to my phone – it's as if I have a speed-devil sitting on my shoulder shouting at me to type a reply as fast as I can.)

Hazel Gale, therapist and author, has a simple recommendation when we need to slow down *in the moment* and be more present. She describes how boxers can get stuck in their head when they're distracted and that this results in sluggishness (slowing down, failing to react) and flightiness (more panicked, messy out of balance). So, she recommends that we try the following exercise.[15]

Champion focus in 30 seconds
To combat the distraction problem, Hazel started teaching boxers a mindfulness technique. She says it isn't her invention (having seen a similar process credited to therapy trainer Russ Harris). She calls it Nine Things, and it involves a series of simple requests.

She advises taking a little time for each step:

Step 1: Without moving your head, notice three things you can see.

Step 2: Notice three things you can hear.

Step 3: Notice three things you can feel in contact with your body.

Step 4: Breathe, go to peripheral vision, and calmly notice all nine things at once.

Hazel explains that this focusing in on the senses forces us to be in the present (and also to slow down). In addition, trying to focus on all nine things consumes our subconscious as it's hard to focus on so many things at once. This in turn interrupts our distracting thoughts.

---

15 https://medium.com/swlh/champion-focus-in-30-seconds-3201afdc10f7

Newsflash: You don't have to answer every email within two minutes

Do you remember those games they used to have at fairgrounds where you had those heads sticking up and you had to bash them with a hammer as quickly as you could to get the highest score?

Well, that's how I feel when I see emails or any types of messages. I want to bash them with a hammer and make them disappear.

This happens more now I'm older (I like to have an empty inbox always or I get anxious) and is not an effective work strategy because replying to an email very quickly is not the name of the game and you don't get awarded any prizes (in fact, quite the opposite, as you can just contribute to chaos and misunderstandings because you haven't been quite thoughtful enough in terms of your response).

So, I need a lesson in boundaries.

In our chat Hazel defines a boundary thus:

> Boundaries can be understood as the lines that exist between you feeling 'okay' and you feeling 'not okay' (which could mean angry, sad, stuck, dejected, frightened, or any other negative emotion). A boundary breach, therefore, is anything that takes you over the line and into a place of 'not okay'.

And if we think about the analogy of the fairground game, instead of bashing each email on the head as quickly as possible, we need to raise the hammer mid-air, let it hover, consider whether bashing it on the head is the right idea and then proceed (and leave some heads well alone – sorry this analogy doesn't really work, does it?).

Can I also suggest that every office has one of those machines in reception so you could vent frustration in your lunch hour by visualising different colleagues' faces while brandishing your hammer (don't you think that would be a good workplace therapy?).

In essence, setting boundaries is becoming more and more important because we are often not working in the same room together, can't see how urgent something is (because in emails and WhatsApp and Slack, everything seems to have an urgency to it), have access to our phones which are happy for us to work 24/7, and we feel pressure to reply if we're working or not working. Setting boundaries is intrinsically linked to slowing things down and not feeling as if our working lives are headed towards an explosion.

Boundaries are important, Hazel explains, because they're intrinsic to self-respect. Without them we quickly feel overwhelmed and out of control:

> They help you to handle challenge, adversity and stress without feeling swamped, and they provide a framework for positive, loving relationships and collaboration. Your boundaries are your integrity and your authenticity. They come from a place of personal strength, and every time you practise living in a boundaried way, you'll feel that strength growing too, because boundaries are not just about holding other people accountable. Being truly boundaried means holding yourself accountable – it's about claiming a sense of power by staying honest, awake, clear and aware.

If we don't set boundaries in terms of the pace we want to work and what we want to take on, others will set them for us. Then we quickly get resentful because we're no longer shaping our own work flow.

Hazel explains why many of us find it hard to get these boundaries established:

> The great irony is that people shy away from stating their boundaries because they don't want to be seen as the villain, or as high maintenance, difficult and so on. But the reality

is quite the opposite: it feels good to be around people who have solid, healthy boundaries because it feels good to know where you stand, and that you can trust someone to be direct. Equally, it feels good to know that you can start to trust yourself to speak up when something feels wrong – to be able to walk away from a challenging situation knowing that you didn't compromise on your own beliefs. Ultimately, boundaries lead the way to love, respect and real, enduring friendship both with other people and with yourself.

So, let's return to the email example that I mentioned earlier. Here's my simple diagram illustrating what not to do when setting boundaries:

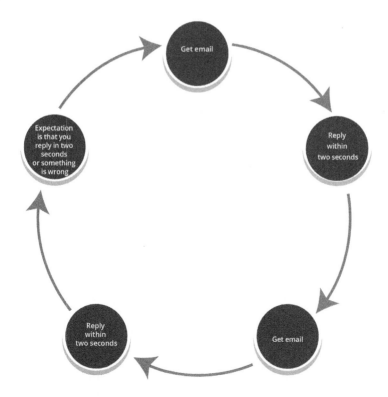

So here what you've done is to set up the expectation that you will always reply to emails within two seconds. Then you get resentful because colleagues start expecting that you'll do this all the time. And that even on your days off you will do it. And that you will do it within two seconds. It's important to remember that just because you see an email doesn't mean you have to reply to it. On your non-working days, it's important that you don't reply (unless of course it's really urgent).

It's funny how hard women find it to do this – to switch off and stop replying, or to not reply so quickly. It's all tied up with our inherent people-pleasing tendencies. It goes against our nature to not try and help or to say no, so we keep getting trapped in work scenarios where we are the ones doing the damage to ourselves.

Here is another diagram to illustrate how to set an effective boundary:

It really can be that simple. When you get an email think:
Do I need to reply straightaway?
Do I need to reply at all?
Or if you think of the head popping up, look at the head, get your hammer ready and then put the hammer down rather than instinctively bashing it just so you can file it away and have an empty inbox.

Here is another useful task designed by Hazel for how to get more in touch with boundaries:

1. Identify a challenging context (e.g. your work, a key relation-ship) and write it at the top of a sheet of paper.

2. Draw a vertical line down the centre of that page, forming two columns for 'not okay' and 'okay'.

3. In the left-hand column (not okay), make a note of the things that trigger a negative emotion for you within your chosen context. These could include practical considerations like how many hours of work is too many for a day, or how far is too far to travel for a meeting. There may also be interpersonal considerations like the ways in which it's not okay for you to be spoken to, or types of tasks you find too challenging to do alone.

4. Finally, for every 'not okay' entry, have a think about what its 'okay' counterpart would be. For example, if it's not okay to work until 8 p.m. in the evening, what would be okay? 7 p.m., 6 p.m., 5 p.m? There are no set rules for these things, which is why boundaries are hard to practise. This all comes down to your personal preferences, needs and circumstances.

Hazel explains that this exercise helps people get in touch with *where* their boundaries are. The next step, she says, is to work out who needs be told about those boundaries and how that information will be best delivered. Hazel also states: 'We don't always get what we originally want. But that doesn't mean we need to settle for some new "not okay" thing. There will almost always be something that can be arranged that feels okay for you. Find it.'

There are many benefits to slowing down. We can be more mindful and less reactive to work communication. We can feel more inspired because we've given our brain time to relax and think about a task. It can also improve the quality of our work. And the idea that faster is always better is definitely not true.

Think about the tortoise who won that race, not the hare.

CHAPTER SIX

Technology: Friend or Annoying Arsehole?

Who would your phone be if it was a person?

Sometimes I think about my phone and try to imagine what they'd be like as a person – a living, breathing person.

My phone would be a man.

They'd be a man who smells heavily of after shave.

A domineering man who never leaves you in peace.

They'd be a man who would be constantly clamouring for your attention.

I am thinking they'd be Mick Jagger circa 1969, wearing a feather boa and tight lurex shorts and clapping in that distinctive manner every two seconds so that each time I tried rest I'd feel drawn towards their presence.

I'd want to touch them.

I'd want to check in with them.

They would be magnetic and a complete arsehole (I haven't met Mick Jagger but I imagine he has these qualities of magnetism and arsehol-ism – many genius musicians have this mix).

The thing is that the phone itself – my phone, your phone, your mum's phone – doesn't have a personality. What it represents is what you allow it to represent but the problem is it contains technology that is designed to get right under your skin. It is drenched in sexy hormones (when I was a teenager there was a fragrance called 'In Musk', and it claimed that if you wore it people would just kiss you in the street, and this is what technology is like – it is irresistible and makes us act in irrational and stupid ways).

For me, in my forties, my phone is both friend and foe. I am not a digital native so I struggle to use it efficiently. It is not intuitive because I didn't grow up with it. I also know what life was like without it (but this is becoming a distant memory). I know that my life has changed in good and bad ways.

Don't create narratives around how crap you are with technology

So, first off let me ban you from saying the words, 'I am no good at technology'. For too long in my career I told myself this. Too many women in their forties and fifties tell themselves that they are no good at tech. The thing is that if you gave a millennial a fax machine and a mobile phone the size of a toaster, they'd struggle too. It's just different ways of doing things. Admittedly, it does feel at times as if the pace of change is intense when it comes to tech but what's important is deciding about the things you need to know about and then pushing away the stuff that you don't need to know about (i.e. you don't need to be an expert in everything). As well as technology, there is often a feeling among women of my generation that they aren't good with numbers. Numbers, technology, science – all these things were more masculine skillsets and so women growing up were told they weren't good at these things (and didn't see examples of women being good at them to inspire them).

I didn't ever engage with numbers in board meetings. Even now I find that when numbers and percentages are being talked about my brain switches off. I managed to conceal my discomfort when I was a managing partner because I had a friend who would talk me through the numbers and make them more digestible, but it still meant that I couldn't get involved in meaningful chat. I was too worried that someone would challenge me on the numbers and my weakness would be exposed.

I was afraid.

This fear is expressed through the diagram below and you can see that if you fear a certain thing – say technology, or numbers – then you avoid learning that thing and so the circle of ineptitude goes on into infinity.

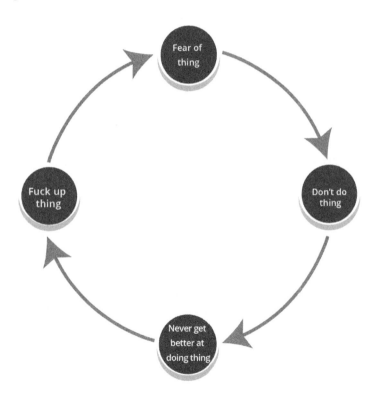

When I was launched into the freelance world and I had to hawk myself, it was no good telling clients that I couldn't do stuff. I had to focus on my positives. This is a *big* lesson to learn for women as we get older: *Whatever the thing is that you can't do, stop telling people that you can't do it. Find someone who can do it and get them to teach you.*

Let colleagues and Google search be your friend

Fast forward to my current role and I found myself working for an app. An app. How was that going to work for someone in their late forties who didn't understand tech? I had night sweats the week before I started. I thought about how I'd be unmasked in a company meeting and the employees would dance around me cackling and shrieking because I had misunderstood some techno-term and was a complete fool. Then I had this sudden epiphany. There was this thing called Google, and when you typed a question into it – any question – it would usually come up with an answer. When someone asked me to 'Put together your growth metric data', instead of vomiting into the toilet with fear I simply Googled it and then found some information to help me write my own version, and I was on my way. I also realised that I could understand numbers. I could understand them when they were communicated in a human way. If someone bamboozled me with numbers then my brain switched off and the familiar narrative haunted me – 'I am not good with numbers' being the main refrain – *but* if someone used numbers to bring an important point to life, using it as evidence to support their point of view, well then I understood them very well. I began to realise that it wasn't that I wasn't good at numbers at all – it was more that the way they'd been used in my past roles was to intimidate me.

They'd been used to shut me up in meetings. So if I came up with a point then some jackass would pull a stat out of their pants and throw it in my face. Or if someone wanted to shout more loudly, they'd use a whole raft of numbers in quick succession to dominate. *Numbers were not the problem.* It was the way they were being used. And they weren't being used to help me do my job.

How to make technology your ally

I spoke to Annie Auerbach, author of *Flex: The Modern Woman's Handbook*, about how technology can be an ally and an enemy. I talked to her about how sometimes it's framed as something that can liberate us (and the fact that we can send urgent emails from the park when we're with the kids can sometimes be a positive) but it can also make us obsessive in terms of our behaviour and so we find it a challenge to switch off.

Annie elaborates on this point:

> The problem is that we can swap the 9 to 5 for 24/7, and the tech means that we are tethered to our work. We're hardwired to twitch to notifications. I worry that we spend more time looking at our phones than our kids', partner's or friends' faces. We need hard edges to our flex, the conviction to switch off emails when we're not working, the strength to leave our phones in another room or a drawer so we spend proper time on concentrated work or happy downtime.

The issue is that we become addicted to checking our phones and so struggle to ever really be present. I found that this behaviour was ramped up even further when working from home because it became more normalised. So, I was putting a wash on while checking emails at the same time, not really doing either thing effectively, or saying, 'Just five minutes' to my youngest daughter and then finding myself scrolling through social media (my job involves managing social media which is dangerous as I am a terrible scroller) and 20 minutes had passed and my daughter had wandered off.

The technology will get into every corner of our life if we let it, so we must set those 'hard edges' that Annie talks about or we risk work bleeding into every area of our life.

And the same is pretty much true with technology at work. If technology gets in the way of you doing your job, then it's useless. If you spend more time filling in your time sheets and workload diaries and task masters and updating your Excel sheets on key metrics than doing your job then it's not helpful. If you spend more time clicking the thumbs-up emoji on Slack just to be present and prove you are on your phone than doing meaningful work then it's not helpful. If you use a platform and it's so complex and un-user-friendly that it gives you a migraine so you never access that information, then it's not helpful.

As Steve Jobs so readily understood, technology is only useful if it helps you. Good tech, good well-designed stuff, should feel easy to use. It should feel intuitive and smooth. It should help with process rather than hinder. And once you get your head round the idea that it's the technology that isn't working and not you not understanding it, then that's a massive leap forward.

So, in summary let me tell you the most important hacks I've learned if you're feeling out of the loop technology wise:

Talk to your colleagues about it and you'll discover that they have problems too – when you're older it can be easy to assume that your technological shitness is related to your age. I've often found that younger colleagues are going through the same stuff as me but have simply got better at Googling, asking for help or being more familiar with alternatives they can use.

Always try and figure something out first rather than flagging up that you can't do it. It's really depressing when your boss sits down with you and you immediately reel off a long list of stuff you can't do. Use the classic 'shit sandwich' feedback technique (I used it for 18 years when giving appraisals). So, you say something like, 'I'm really excited to be using the Spud18 platform as it looks pretty cool but I am finding it a challenge to get the password right as it changes every two days apparently. Can I talk to IT to see if there is something easy we can do to help with that?'

Breathe. My gut instinct when I am faced with something I don't understand is to stop breathing. I hold my breath. Then I start to breathe very rapidly. Then I stop. Basically, these are not helpful things as it means you feel as if you're going to faint. Instead, take a short walk outside. Try a couple of breathing techniques out and then look at the thing when you've calmed down. Google it. If that doesn't work, find a colleague and talk to them about it.

Don't keep saying negative age-related stuff to other people. Instead of saying, 'I'm so old that I can't do this stuff' or, 'I must be really out of date as I can't understand this,' just shut up and say nothing. Ask for support but stop the self-deprecating thing. Think about what Madonna/Oprah/Beyoncé would do when faced with the same situation. They wouldn't even bother with the self-deprecation. They would just get on with it or if they really struggled then they'd delegate. That is another thing you can do if the person isn't overwhelmed and you're doing some sort of trade (i.e. 'I will do this if you can please log into the Spud18 platform because I have changed my password so many times that my computer screen has frozen.')

Don't do stuff very quickly and make mistakes. Sometimes I find that the speed of communications now – what with Slack messaging and the like – means that I just send messages without reading what I'm replying to. A recent example:

Boss: Have you replied to the message on social media?

Me: (not looking at screen grab): Yes, I do all the Instagram ones but not Twitter

Boss: This one is from Instagram

Me: Oh, I have done them all (then looking at the screen grab and realising that I haven't replied to these). Oh no, I haven't

Boss: So, have you done them or not?

Me: No

Correct dialogue:

Boss: Have you replied to the message on social media?

Me: (looking at screen grab for a few seconds:) I will do these right away. Thanks for the update.

Some technology is super useful and there are some skills you need to nurture. Annie gave me the lowdown on the most important skills when it comes to tech (the ones that we need to get busy with if we can't do them already):

1. **Write clearly so your messages and meaning aren't misinterpreted.** Annie states, 'This clearly is a skill which we will have to develop as we rely more and more on instant communication. So many emails are lost in translation. We need to write with clarity and without ambiguity.' And a note from me here, based on years of more 'analogue' work experience. I've mentioned this before but it's worthwhile picking up the phone and talking to someone if you worry that your message may be taken the wrong way. Some people hate phone calls, yes, but a two-minute conversation is so much easier than ping-ponging back and forth via email and then you both getting the wrong end of the stick.

2. **Learn how to get the most out of Zoom meetings, even if you hate them.** You need to be able to get the most out of these meetings because they're not going anywhere. Annie says:

Getting everyone on the same page at the start of meetings is important. People have probably jumped from one meeting into the next so allow a breather at the beginning for everyone to re-orientate themselves and understand the purpose of what you're doing. Also notice who is speaking and who isn't – be empathetic and seek out opinions from the introverts instead of letting the same old voices dominate the Zoom as they would the room.

3. **Ensure that people working from home don't get left out of the important decisions.** Include remote works and physically present workers in calls and meetings – make sure proximity doesn't breed favouritism and those working remotely are not out of sight, out of mind.

At the end of the day, there will always be changes in terms of the technology we use. If you gave a young person a fax machine and asked them to send off some faxes right away, they'd struggle. You learned how to use a Nutribullet, right? And you learned how to post on Instagram. And you probably have learned how to do a reel and point your finger at different titles (which seems to be what everyone does these days). You can adapt to new technology.

You will learn.

We can make technology work for us. It can be on our side but the first step is telling ourselves that we can navigate it, that we can use it to our advantage. Once we do that we can *take over the world* (cue mad cackling and a close up of a woman throwing her head back in a maniacal manner).

The Flow: How It's a Very Good Thing

Let it flow
Just let yourself flow
Slow and low
That is the tempo

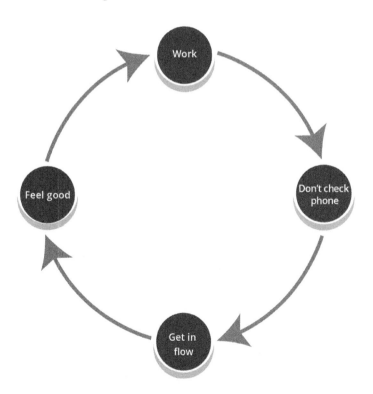

This is an amended lyric from an old Beastie Boys song that I used to listen to when I was growing up. It makes me think about the best times at work, when you feel absorbed in what you're doing, time slips away and you don't notice the world around you and you feel in that moment that you are really achieving your goals. When you finish, you make an audible sigh and do the kind of face that Michelangelo would have done after he'd just completed a really good painting of a hand and got all the fingers looking right and not like a bunch of bananas (this is how I paint hands unfortunately).

Flow.

You get it in yoga.

In dancing.

When you have great sex (if you can remember that far back).

Flow is when work doesn't feel as if it takes up lots of effort. It's when your ideas are just coming out and you're getting stuff done. It's when you are not side-tracked by lots of bitty tasks and admin and you get a sense of accomplishment.

Here's some tips on how to get into that flow state (that work for me):

- Use an app on your phone that stops you looking at your phone – something like Forest, which stops you from looking at social media and you kill a tree if you pick your phone up and try and browse. Or just hide your phone downstairs.
- Set a timer and tell yourself that you won't check emails or Slack or any other messaging services for at least 45 minutes.
- Put some music on your headphones. I find it hard to get into flow with music but sometimes classical music can help, as long as it's not too loud and doesn't have big,

operatic voices that distract me as I try to figure out what they're singing about.

- Be comfortable in your seat and not distracted by your knickers being up your bum.
- Have something inspiring to stare at when you look up from your laptop. Now, I am staring at a lovely fabric banner my friend sent me which says, 'You've got this.'
- Don't pick up your phone (again, this is just a reminder but it really won't help).
- Congratulate yourself when you've completed the task or at least got really stuck into it – write it down as one your achievements (remembering that this helps fight the imposter syndrome).

CHAPTER SEVEN

How to Be a Working Parent and
Say Fuck Off to Guilt

Gibbering wreck status is normal

First off, let me preface this chapter by saying that there will be times when you're a gibbering wreck. This chapter title should be 'How to Work as a Gibbering Wreck Parent'. This is just the reality of parenting and working. Some parents manage to conceal this more than others. However, the minute you open up at work to another parent you will find that a cascade of worries/guilt/pain comes out of their mouth and you connect because you realise that we are often all in the same collective boat.

The pandemic was rough on everyone but mothers found themselves at home, trying to work, and home-school or look after small children at the same time.

A *Financial Times* survey[16] revealed that two out of five working mothers had taken or were considering taking a step back from work because they were finding it impossible to juggle work and childcare. Seventy per cent of working mothers said they felt that household duties fell to them, with almost the same amount saying they failed to manage more than an hour of uninterrupted work. This had a direct impact on their mental health – dealing

16 www.ft.com/content/d5d01f06-9f7c-4cdc-9fee-225e15b5750b

with the stress of looking after children and trying to navigate an ever-changing working from home dynamic.

For many, it became relentless. In an office, there is some freedom in that parents aren't expected to walk straight from a meeting into changing a nappy, then trying to work out how to dial into a maths Zoom with a dodgy iPad. The pandemic illustrated how trying to work and parent at the same time cannot be done.

Even in normal times, parenting is a tough gig. There is so much judgement. So many expectations. The reality is that if you want to work, putting the TV on for long periods of time is going to be your only option. Yet none of us admit that this is what we do because we're worried that people will think we're uncaring, rubbish parents.

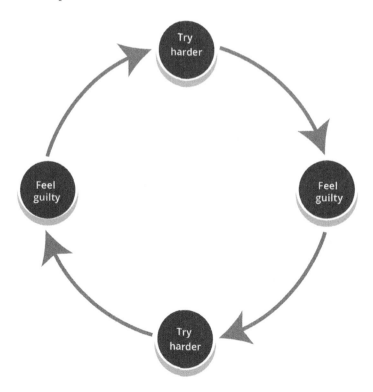

This diagram represents what happens when you are trying to be a perfect parent – it is what happens because society has made parenting a thing that we must achieve and pass our exams in. It is no longer about feeding the child and helping the child navigate life. It is all about ensuring the child does not ever feel any unpleasantness in their entire life.

Once you realise that you can never ensure this, that you will sometimes be a source of unpleasantness and that you can't achieve perfection (at work or as a parent), then things become much easier.

There were two massive issues that came up for me once I became a parent. No, make that three massive issues:

- Guilt.
- No time for myself.
- Exhaustion.

No, hang on, there were four because there was also *childcare*. And let's look at them individually as if it's some sort of working parent beauty contest – but these issues aren't entirely beautiful because they result in quite a lot of stress and there aren't any easy answers.

In my online survey, many women said that they no longer wanted to work at the breakneck speed that they'd worked before kids; 47.5 per cent said they wanted to slow down and 32.5 per cent said they didn't want to try and achieve all the time because it was simply too much. Some of this is also related to coming out of a pandemic and experiencing a shaking up of our priorities – we are perhaps re-evaluating what we want from life and when work and kids are placed side by side we realise that we want to prioritise kids more.

Guilt

Parenting generally is something that we feel guilty about. We shouldn't but it's because parenting is a thing that we are supposed to be good at, perfect even, and in the early days we try as best we can to do everything right (whatever that means) and then start dropping balls because there is no such thing as right. There is only really what works for you (aside from ensuring your kids eat, sleep, wear sunscreen and so on, that is). When you throw going back to work into the mix then you have this layer of feeling guilty because you aren't with them, or you miss their bedtime or you worry that the patchwork quilt of childcare arrangements isn't working or that you don't bake with them or make any World Fuck Day kids outfits and buy a shit one online instead each year. Social media is both a blessing and a curse – if you follow the right people then it's a source of reassurance but if you inadvertently follow someone who is a parenting show off then you can suddenly feel an overwhelming sense of guilt.

I remember when I realised, quite early on, that I was never going to be the mum in a Cath Kidston pinafore, baking cakes and smiling inanely at my children. The thing is, we often model our parenting on our own parents and my mum wasn't one of these baking, crafting, perfection lovers either. She rode a moped, had a nose piercing and pink hair. She was a good mother but work was important to her and so was her life outside her children.

I am the same. Work is not only important to me, it's a necessity because I support our family on my income (and my partner helps a lot with childcare but isn't the main breadwinner). Nonetheless, I would choose to work even if I didn't have to work. I need it. I need it to stay sane. Sometimes I feel guilty about this too – should I gain all my identify and satisfaction from being a mother? How come I get bored when I'm playing with my children? And bored in the park pushing them on the swings? Why do I often find myself tuning out and fantasising about when I can next sit down and do some writing? Yes, if you choose to feel guilty then there is a veritable smorgasbord of stuff to feel guilty about. Take your pick.

I am going to mention Mel Robbins and her book *The High 5 Habit*, again. Mel talks about how we get stuck in a negative chain of thought and can't get out. This is often how I feel when guilt sets in. I feel guilt and then find a whole host of parenting mistakes I've made that day to add to the guilt. Her simple technique is to simply call time on negative thinking patterns by saying the words, 'I'm not thinking about that now', and shutting that voice up. This has been working well for me. If there are occasions when you feel as if you've stepped out of line and need to apologise to your child (like shouting fits, which I am definitely prone to) then make sure you take the time to explain your feelings, why you're feeling them and how it's normal for parents to feel angry, just like everyone else. Then stop beating yourself up about it. A great parenting book that I'd recommend is *The Book You Wish Your Parents Had Read (And Your Children Will Be Glad You Did)* by Philippa Perry, which has lots of practical and non-guilt-inducing parenting tips inside.

No time for myself ever in my whole life, not ever

In the noughties, people called this 'juggling' and there were lots of interviews with high-flying finance women with hundreds of children who chuckled about it and seemed to be doing it rather well. Juggling sounds fun. It isn't. Juggling is headache-inducing and makes your stomach hurt. It's not what clowns do to entertain people – it's the feeling that your head is going to explode because you're running around Waterloo station trying to source a children's present for a party and some wrapping paper and you've just missed the train that will get you home to see your kids before they go to bed. It's the feeling when you turn up to school and it's Crazy Ass Sock Day for no reason and you've forgotten and your kid is weeping because you are trying to send a presentation from your phone via Google Drive but the password has changed from %^&$£*()QQW to @!£$RF^&*

So, let's call it transitioning, which sounds slightly better.

We have our work selves and then we have our mum selves and they are often quite different.

You may find yourself at work sometimes saying, 'Mummy is just going to the toilet' to your colleague or wiping some stray sandwich off their cheek with the corner of a hankie that you've spat on, but it's likely that your two identities are quite different. The trickiest aspect of working and motherhood is moving from one identity to the other. At worst, you are the person hunched over your phone grunting in the park while your kid falls off a slide and the other mums judge you. At best, it's a muddle. Compromise. It's taking a deep breath before you get home – sometimes wanting to just lie on the path instead of going in because you know that when you get in, the chaos and mess and noise and needs will be overwhelming.

You will feel very tired for long periods of time (exhaustion)

There is nothing much to say about this challenge. Anybody who says that raising children and working isn't exhausting is on drugs. Or they have a nanny. Or they are on drugs and have a nanny. It is worse when they are small and you're not getting any sleep and having to cart them about the place. It's more mentally fraught when they're teenagers and you're paranoid about whether they're secretly sending photos of their bums on Snapchat or selling weed to their school mates while you've taken your eye off the ball and haven't noticed.

For me, I had to give up drinking. I had to give it up and I had to take a lot of supplements. I knew that I couldn't drink, have a bad diet, bring up children and work in a demanding job without having a nervous breakdown due to extreme tiredness. When you're tired, it is impossible to be creative, or productive, or even see things in a rational way.

I also do the morning routine and make sure I exercise three times a week – even if it's just jumping around the kitchen for half an hour. I rely on caffeine, which I know isn't healthy, BUT I NEED SOME SORT OF VICE, OKAY?

NB: In fact, you can't even read this book if you're tired so put it down and get some sleep if you need it, right?

Childcare (and flexible working)

This is the massive issue when you're going back to work. The rough estimate for sending a child to nursery full time per week is £263.00. If you have more than one small kid then you will struggle because it may work out that your entire salary is going on childcare.

It means that many women simply can't afford to work and their careers stop until they get some subsidised childcare or their kids are of school age. Then when school starts, there are still the outside school hours which don't match office hours. There are plenty of excellent articles and books about these things but the reality is that it's very hard to find a job that pays well and offers flexibility. It is hard to be senior in an organisation and be flexible because we haven't caught up with the concept that you can work around a different time schedule and still be productive. If it makes you feel any better, research has revealed that in an average eight-hour working day a person is usually productive for about two hours and 53 minutes. A study of 2000 full-time workers revealed that they were immersed in a whole load of unproductive activities, which included reading news websites, browsing social media, discussing non-work-related activities with colleagues and searching for new jobs.[17]

So, you can quote this stat at your employer when you are asking for a more flexible work schedule – full-time hours do not equate with meaningful work for all that time. If you're productive for three hours then you are doing just as well as your full-time colleagues.

For many women, it means that they must take a far less senior position to get the flexibility they need. This is what happened to me and it's happened to just about every woman I've worked with. The only women who stayed at the very top of the organisation I used to work for were wealthy enough to have nannies but this meant they often suffered with the guilt thing because they didn't feel they were spending enough time with their kids.

So, all this stuff – the exhaustion, the lack of affordable child-care, lack of flexibility, challenge of transitioning from one identity to another, the exhaustion – these are all things that come up before you've even actually looked at the work itself. Then we add in office politics, the ceaseless pace, less of a boundary between work and home, women taking on more domestic admin, being responsible for making World Fuck Day costumes at the drop of a hat, and then having passive aggressive WhatsApp messages pinged at them 24/7 about more meaningless but seemingly important admin and chores means that many working mums are pissed off. Grumpy, angry and fed up, and that's before they've even sat down at their desks. Before they've got the email from a colleague which critiques the colour they've used on the left-hand box of the presentation because it's not 'magenta enough'. Before they've had to sit in a meeting and listen to someone talk about how they got sunburn because they fell asleep in the sun for 12 hours on the beach (and

---

17 www.inc.com/melanie-curtin/in-an-8-hour-day-the-average-worker-is-productive-for-this-many-hours.html

try not to scream WHEN DO I GET TO FALL ASLEEP IN THE DAYTIME YOU FUCKING CRETIN? WHEN DO I GET TO DO THAT?). Many women have done four hours of work before they walk through the office door.

Before I had kids, I used to look at working mums coming into the office and this would be my internal monologue.

Shit, she hasn't even brushed her hair this morning. She's got the same skirt on she had on yesterday. Boden. Why do they all wear BODEN? And why is there a baby wipe stuck to her flip flop? Didn't she get the memo about not wearing open-toed sandals in the office? Who doesn't have time to smear Touche Éclat under their eyes? It's nine 9.45 and she's yawning! I've been to the gym and had a hot shower and answered all these mails and she'd not even replied to the one I sent an hour ago. And she probably wants to leave early. And she was super aggressive when I told her about that magenta box that wasn't the right colour in the PowerPoint doc. She practically bit my head off. Then yesterday her tummy was rumbling when we were on the conference call! It's funny, I noticed she rarely gets up from her desk. She's probably on Facebook sharing photos of her kids. I guess she could be working. I mean she does seem to work hard. She told me to leave her alone when I wanted to talk about Fleabag and I was only trying to get bants going. She hadn't even heard of the Dim Sum restaurant in Soho that I was chatting about. She looked as if she'd been crying again.

The other thing that we aren't particularly good at as women (see Chapter Three on the broken fucking cup) is having a few moments where we are not working/not looking after children/not doing something useful. When I speak to mothers, I am always struck by how they fill up their time with stuff – be it tidying, putting washing away, child admin, sorting – so this means that every moment of time is filled with activity. Working from home initially sounded like a good idea for mothers but for many of us the typical day morphed into the following:

6 a.m.: Put wash on, empty dishwasher, make beds.

7 a.m.: Get kids ready, get self ready, get stuff out of freezer for dinner.

8 a.m.: School run, check emails, do a small shop, get back to kitchen table for work.

9 a.m.–12 p.m.: Work Zooms, work admin, reply to WhatsApp messages about upcoming 'World Book Day,' costume sale

12–1 p.m.: Put clothes away while eating a sandwich and trying to find a pair of cycling shorts for PE day, notice cobwebs in bathroom and spend ten minutes dusting as notice entire house is full of cobwebs

1–3 p.m.: Work, calls, Slack, more work.

3–4 p.m.: School run while checking emails.

4–6 p.m.: Finish off work with children in the background, put dinner on, arrange for one kid to be taken to Brownies and get locked into a chat for 20 minutes and miss an important email.

6–10 p.m.: Dinner, bedtime, spend 'quality time' with kids but they're grumpy and tired, bath time, collapse on sofa, scroll through work channels to see what has been missed, as invariably something has, load dishwasher, feed cats, wipe kitchen floor, watch TV.

Does this sound like you too? When we work from home, we need to fight the urge to do domestic stuff and admin in and among our working day. Or at least try not to do it all the time. We need to fight the urge to tidy while we work. Simply ask yourself – if you were in the office, would you spend half an hour in your lunch break crawling under the office table to clear up crumbs that a colleague had dropped on the floor? No, you would probably spend that time answering emails but the point is you'd not feel compelled to combine work and chores as much as you do at home because you'd not be working in your messy house – you'd be away from it, which is no bad thing. I hope that as hybrid working becomes normalised we will get used to being at home and won't feel the pressure of constantly tidying up. It is useful to just say the words *this can wait till another time* if you notice that there's blue toothpaste stuck all over the bathroom taps. Make sure you take breaks and do nothing when working from home. Don't feel bad if you make a tea that is leftovers or from the freezer.

Remember that you can't do everything perfectly at all times without your head exploding. Think about the permission slip earlier in the book and write yourself one for when you're working from home.

This slip gives you permission to not do any domestic stuff during your work day and to remind yourself that you wouldn't be doing it if you were in the office so it wouldn't be getting done and therefore doesn't need to be getting done in this particular moment.

A Transitioning Tip – From Work Mode to Parenting Mode

If you're a parent there is often that moment when you've got the tube and the bus home and your brain is still jittery with all the stuff you've done at work – the meetings, the things you didn't accomplish, maybe a chunk of critique from your boss which sits like an undigested rusk in your stomach – and you stand on the doorstep about to put your key in the door and are mentally trying to prepare yourself for what will be inside.

CHAOS.
NOISE.
SHOUTING.

(This is if you have young kids. If they're older then you may be met with silence but that can be worrying in its own way too.)

For a moment, you may consider turning your back and just sitting on the wall outside your house for a few moments longer. I had a colleague and she used to laugh as I raced to get home so I could put my youngest to bed.

'Why don't you miss bedtime altogether?' she said. 'Bedtime is the worst time of the day, isn't it?'

It's true that I don't massively enjoy quality time at the end of the day because I'm tired and the kids are tired but I also have this voice whispering in my ear and it usually says, *'You've been out all day and haven't seen them so how could you miss this precious interlude while they shout in your face and you try and forget all the stuff you didn't achieve today and sing John Denver's 'Leaving on a Jet Plane"* (Mum sang it to me when I was a baby. I think she had yearnings to leave the family at home and fly off somewhere more peaceful perhaps.)

So, okay, one thing you could do is kick guilt to the kerb and leave bedtime to your other half for once. There is nothing wrong with this. There is no certificate that is awarded for completing every single bedtime of your child's life. So, you could let that bus fly past as you commute home, put a podcast on, sup a ginger beer and just stare at your feet for an extra 20 minutes (but you'll feel guilty because we are socially conditioned to always feel as if we've done something wrong). The other tip to ease this transition is to walk in, brace yourself, remind yourself that you are powerful and are basically amazing and can do anything, and pour yourself a large glass of cool water. Take your shoes off. Don't look at the mess or the chaos or the fact that the cat is covered in Peppa Pig stickers and is running in terror up the stairs.

Invest in a nice dressing gown. (I'm not joking when I tell you I have about ten dressing gowns – they are high street and are all silky fabric and make me feel as if I'm about to go on stage in the West End. I'm not a fan of towelling ones that make me feel as if I'm about to kick the bucket any moment.)

Splash some water on your face.

Get one of those calming sprays and spritz it all over the place.

Dump the critique from earlier and remind yourself you can worry about it some more in the morning but now is the time for family and maybe Netflix (family and Netflix are my life).

Breathe.

Go downstairs.

You are strong.

Say the words, 'I am great. I am great. I am great.'

Then sing John Denver until the chaos abates and the children are asleep.

I spoke to Annie Ridout, an author and entrepreneur who runs a successful business offering online courses. She has also written a book called *The Freelance Mum*, which is in the Resources section at the end of this book. We discussed how she navigates parenting and work, and she points out that there aren't any easy solutions. Annie says:

> I actually found the really early months with my babies easiest, in terms of being able to write. They would snooze a lot in the bouncer, and I'd get my head down. Maybe the hormones suited me too, as I felt like the tiredness didn't really hit me so much directly after the birth. As they became more awake and then started moving around – sitting up and then crawling – it became harder. By this point, the tiredness had taken over and sleep deprivation can really affect motivation (and confidence). So, after a particularly bad night's sleep, I always tried to go slowly, and reduce the to-do list. I found using those days for more boring admin tasks was better than trying to get creative. People often said to me: take at least three months off. But I actually felt that working in those first three months was fine, and I should have taken the second three months off. Everyone's experience is different, though, and for some people there needs to be a longer recovery period and proper time away from work.

The transitioning between mum to work and back again is something she also struggles with, and when you're trying to work with kids present (and not doing either well). This scenario often leads to overwhelm for her. Annie says:

I know that when I try to work around my kids, we all get very frustrated. I'll think, *I'll just do a quick Instagram post or email*, and as soon as the laptop opens, all three children will flock to me, talk non-stop and make it completely impossible. It's hard when the inspiration lands and you want to get into that 'flow' state with your work but your kids have other ideas. So, I try hard to separate work and kids. That's not to say I never check my phone around them – I do – but I know my limitations and that proper work can't be done with any child in the vicinity. So, I wait until they're at school and nursery before really getting stuck in. Except sometimes, when I forget the above and attempt to parent and work at the same time. And it always ends badly.

Many mothers will recognise this tendency to try and maximise time so end up working while the kids are around. In lockdown, this was particularly bad, with many of us working and home-schooling at the same time and feeling as if we weren't getting anything right.

One important thing is to try and fight the desire to multi-task (unless you have a work emergency or a child emergency and must do both in that moment). There are times when you can find yourself in a sort of child/work limbo – for me this is when I do the school run on days when I'm working from home. I feel guilty – not because my employer has told me off but because I feel that I should be working rather than picking up the children. Then when I'm with the children, I feel guilty because I keep looking at my phone. What I'm trying to get better at (and it's a work in progress) is putting my phone away when I pick up the kids and dedicating that time to them so I can then return to work later, and there is some separation.

I also know that if I have something important happening workwise and I'm working from home, I must take myself off to the shed. More on the shed later but up until recently I worked from my bed as we have a small house and there was nowhere else I could hide away from the children.

Annie also talks about how we need to recognise when we're running low on energy and try and take proper time off. This might not always be possible if you're in the middle of a big project or have started a new job, but it's important to put some time in your diary in the future so you know you have a break coming up:

> I also feel overwhelmed when I'm tired. I'm usually tired but sometimes it becomes too much and I feel I can't cope. In those periods, I take proper time off. I stop working altogether for a few days – or weeks – and allow myself to recover before hitting burnout.

Annie also sets boundaries for herself. Not all women can do this of course, as it's very much dependent on the kind of work you're doing, but to survive long term as a working parent, you need to be realistic about your workload and fight the urge to take on as much as you physically can.

She ring-fences weekends as a time when she's not going to work:

> I don't work weekends anymore. I did, for a long time, as I didn't have much childcare in the week and I was working hard to build various businesses, as well as my profile as a journalist and author. But now I'm condensing my working week into three days, 9 a.m. to 3 p.m., and trying to enjoy just being with my kids outside those hours. The plan, going forward, is to have all school holidays off (13 weeks a year). We want to get a camper van and travel the UK and Europe during the holidays. It's taken six years of hard graft to get to a stage where I'm earning money more easily, which means this is now looking more feasible.

So here are some tips if you're parenting and working:

- You will often have to compromise.
- You will sometimes make mistakes.
- As much as possible, try and either be in work mode or parenting mode – trying to do both is stressful and means you will probably fuck up.
- Be mindful that colleagues without kids won't always understand why your hair is standing on end and you are crying in the toilet – you were like them back in the day.
- Try to remember that guilt is normal.
- Remember that it's great for your kids to see you working and to see you going after your dreams.
- Talk about stuff when you're going through a stressful time – apologise if you're moody and distracted.
- And finally, if you feel yourself becoming overwhelmed with all those tell-tale physical symptoms – and feeling mentally not quite right too of course – just breathe. Breathe and stop. This is not a race.

Getting Feedback That You Don't Like and Dealing With It

When I was younger, I used to focus on any piece of negative feedback about myself and spend days, weeks even, ruminating on this. My typical pattern went like this:

- Receive piece of criticism (usually in an appraisal).
- Fight back tears while nodding head, unable to contain emotions and finally convinced that all the negative things about me were true.
- Get drunk with colleagues and move on to the next phase, which was usually denial and fury.
- Endure insomnia and nights and nights of creating mock arguments and defences – the things I should have said to defend myself but was too shocked to say at the time.

Now, thankfully, I have got (slightly) better at receiving negative feedback. Instead of letting it take me down a wormhole of self-loathing, I try and do the following:

- Receive piece of criticism.
- Listen to it properly and continue breathing (fighting the urge to cry and remembering that this is part and parcel of work life and not the end of the world).
- Nod head and ask for an example of this particular behaviour/thing.
- While nodding, ask these questions to myself – is it valid? Is it fair? Was it something I was already aware of but hoping nobody would bring up? Is it something I can learn from?

- Acknowledge mistake/criticism and think about what I need to put in place to stop it from happening again (do I need more support/training? Do I need to slow down?).
- Move on.

The important thing I've noticed (as I get older) is that *if* the criticism is unjustified (i.e. there is no practical evidence or the thing wasn't well briefed in or it wasn't something I was responsible for), I am *much* better at calling this out. This isn't about being defensive. This is more about speaking up for yourself. If, in the moment, you feel that the point isn't fair then it's important to give yourself a bit of time; don't respond right away, but go away and think about what they've said and then come back when you've had time to digest it. One of the most mature things to do (rather than get lost in slagging the person off and trying to discredit them) is to write down three or four ways you could avoid it happening again and send this to the person to illustrate that you've taken what they've said on board. The key thing is removing the emotion from it as much as possible. And if it's fair and just, learn from it. None of us is perfect and we can all improve. Don't catastrophise. Don't beat yourself up. Move forward.

CHAPTER EIGHT

Too Old for This Shit: Dealing With Bad Behaviour at Work

It often feels like same old same old when it comes to people

As you get older, you feel as if you're living the same work life over and over. The personality types wear different outfits (and even these come in and out of fashion every five years) but they don't vary much.

In my old work life, much of my time was taken up with managing people. I was the 'People Person', which was shorthand for the only person who had patience to sit and listen to people in their appraisals while they complained about their role/their team/their life. I absorbed a lot of that energy and left most days bent over double with my knuckles scraping along the pavement. During my 18 years' managing and working with people I learned a few things. One of the most important things was this:

- Some are good at what they do and are fun to be around.
- Some are good at what they do and are shit to be around.
- Some are rubbish at what they do and fun to be around.
- Some people are shit at what they do and are shit to be around.

So, in any well-functioning business you ideally want the first type of people – the ones who are talented and good to be around. These are the *radiators*. The ones that people feel inspired by. They are the natural leaders. They are also rare. Many of the people I worked with were what could perhaps be termed as 'geniuses' (in the market research world that is, although many of them believed they were Einstein and weren't) but they had very poor people skills.

In many commercial organisations, a lack of empathy or team skills is acceptable if the individual is generating lots of money. So, you will often see that big business winners with an appalling track record in terms of making people cry and feel miserable aren't challenged because they are cash cows.

These are the people who are good at what they do but are rubbish to be around and long term they have a toxic impact on company culture and will end up costing money because there will be more resignations, more people calling in sick and more time spent moping all the emotional damage.

The third type – the ones who are rubbish at the job but nice to be around – at least make the team feel good when they're in the room but the problem is that they naturally create more work. However, these kinds of people are rare – there is usually something they can do that is helpful workwise.

Finally, the rubbish/shit people. These people are everywhere in the world of work. They may not be rubbish permanently. They may be in the wrong job or going through some awful stuff in their life.

Overall, I would say that I've usually fallen into the first type and the third. The common trait is *I hope* that I've been good to be around. In fact, the reason that I was often not very good at my job was because I was too focused on others and let that get in the way of what I was doing (or was too worried to fess up that I couldn't do something for fear that they'd tell me off or judge me).

What I'm saying is that being someone who is 'good to be around' is a massively great quality at work. It means that people want to work with you because it's pleasant. The thing is that you need to not let the being 'good to be around' bit get in the way of you doing your job – so also be confident enough to ask for help and support, or to delegate.

I have read a lot of different theories of different personality types at work. If we park the 'radiator' versus 'drain' analogy or the 'good to be around' versus 'rubbish to be around', I think the additional categories are probably straightforward. These are:

- jerks
- arseholes
- twerps
- show-offs
- sexist pigs
- dinosaurs
- lazy bastards
- tossers
- creeps
- wankers
- bitches
- cold-hearted liars
- beasts.

You can add your own list (and let me tell you this is a great therapy if you've had a bad day at work – simply write down a load of terms to describe the person who has driven you mad and it feels mighty cathartic and cleansing).

I apologise as most of these terms possibly refer more to the men I've worked with rather than the women (I came from a particularly masculine, sexist work culture). You probably have your own list somewhere and feel free to add to my scientific categories. One thing that comes with age is the ability to spot these different categories of people straightaway. And another thing that I've learned is that it doesn't matter how clever you are, or how good you are at your job, if you're a twerp and a sexist then nobody will enjoy working with you, you will end up upsetting people and contributing to a toxic work culture and ultimately the company performance will be impacted.

I used to interview lots of people for roles and was surprised by just how much importance was placed on where they went to university and ultimately how 'clever' they were (whatever that means, as we can all be clever at different things).

So, the interview process would go something like this:

'Oh I see you went to Oxford/Cambridge. Do you know Nancy Smithson-Baith-Wright? She studied in the same year as you?'

'Yes, I did. Yes, I did know Nancy too.'

'Okay, well, we love you and you've got the job.'

Instead what should have been the process:

'Now I am giving you a hypothetical situation – you see a colleague who is struggling with their workload and has stayed late several nights in a row and seems to be crying in the toilets. What do you do?'

'I would ignore them because I am so clever and they are obviously weak or have children or are too old to deal with the challenge of modern work environments.'

'Okay tossbag. Pack your bag. You've failed this interview.'

So it's worth thinking about the kind of person you are at work and which category you fit into. Also, consider if you're hiring someone whether they're going to help you build a positive culture or whether you're going to spend a lot of time mopping up the emotional fallout and wishing you'd never taken them on.

The radiator or the drain. The jerk or the saviour. Of course, it's not always that clear cut and it's also true that the older we get, the more impatient we can be with colleagues. We can also jump to conclusions (see the point on jerks and twats earlier). So, we might walk in and someone is being a bit cocky and because we've been around the work block a few times we dismiss them as a stereotype. It's important that we stop ourselves for a moment. Remind ourselves that while it's helpful to categorise when you're trying to find your feet and navigate the office and its politics, it's unhelpful to jump to conclusions. The most important thing is that we provide a role model to others. So, we don't want to be the grumpy old bitch in the corner who groans whenever someone starts photographing their lunch. It's better if we can collaborate with and help colleagues. Also remember that we are all human. There are often reasons why people behave as they do. If someone is being an arsehole, perhaps they've just had a bad day. Perhaps it's not permanent.

Or perhaps it is.

But ultimately, skill alone is not important. Your ability to get others on board and work as a team really is.

No more Mrs Nice

When I was young, I put up with a lot of very toxic behaviour at work – bullying, arrogance, power games, all sorts of shit – but now that I'm the ripe old age of 48, I won't tolerate it. I had an experience where I started working with a woman who was only what I can describe as… a monster. She didn't start out being a monster. In fact, when I joined her small company, she sent me some nice chocolates and a coffee cup with her company logo on. It was only a few weeks down the line that she started micro-managing everything I did. She would make changes to a presentation while I was amending the changes she'd already requested. She used technology to ensure that every hour of my day was booked up with stuff. She never pointed out anything positive about my work and preferred instead to focus on small, petty details. The work itself was tedious, which didn't help, but the fact that she never praised, never made me feel good about anything I'd contributed took me to a dark place. Initially, I thought it was me. I thought that maybe the fact I'd lost my dad recently, that we were during a pandemic, that my youngest was not even two… I thought all these things meant I wasn't operating at the right level. Then I took a step back and saw that the work I was delivering was good. I also thought about all the times I'd done great work and how other clients and people I'd worked with had been impressed. I worked for her for a few months and quit when she bullied me into working on a project that I wasn't available for. The minute I resigned I felt nothing but relief. Then a couple of months later I met someone else who'd worked with her and had had very similar experiences.

The lesson to all of this? If someone consistently criticises your work, you dread seeing them or speaking to them and they overload you with tasks without mercy, then you need to stand your ground. Be brave and set boundaries. It might not work. This person may be so embedded in the organisation that you find an absence of any support around you. It is definitely worth trying to have that conversation, though, and ultimately it will leave you feeling more empowered. The regrets I have in my work life often revolve around not saying how I felt when I was being bullied by colleagues and even now, years later, I have mock arguments in my head with these self-same colleagues and imagine myself telling them in no uncertain terms how their behaviour impacted on my mental health at the time. There is also the option to find another job but you will be cross with yourself if you allow a bully/ manipulative arse to dictate your work life. Remember that you will always find another job. You are great. They are the arsehole.

Write it on a mirror where you can see it. Remind yourself each day.

I see you, what you did back there was good, well done

This bit of advice is very simple. If you want to nurture good relationships with your team and you want to make them feel good and you want to engender respect then make sure you always tell them when they do something good.

This isn't about using people or trying to influence them (though let's face it, flattery can get you anywhere), it's more about acknowledging that the people you work with are complex beings who have a whole load of their own baggage that they're carrying about all day and while they may come across as having it all sussed, the reality is that they had to commute into work that morning, spilt coffee down their trousers, couldn't find their pen in the meeting so had to pretend to take notes with a blunt pencil and were possibly awake for four hours worrying about things that might go wrong that day. All of us are human. Some of us are wankers but most us are not. So, if you see good work, if you see something that makes you smile because it's clever then take the time to say to them, 'That's brilliant. Well done.'

One of my favourite work phrases is the word 'perfect'. I say it about 17 times a day. I must be careful about how many times I say it but the thing is that word is so reassuring, it says to the other person – I see you, you are good, I salute you, all is well. Try it out and you'll see.

The other area that becomes more challenging to navigate the longer we work is anger. This is especially true if we are also trying to cope with hormonal changes that can make us feel angrier than we ordinarily would. Anger can feel very debilitating and it's something that women rarely talk about for fear of being judged.

How to navigate feeling angry at work

When I reflect on all the times I felt truly out of control in a work environment it was often because I was angry:

- Angry because a colleague had criticised my work.
- Angry because someone else had taken credit for work I'd done.
- Angry at the sexism I saw all around me.
- Angry at the arrogance of some of my colleagues.
- Angry at staying late because there was a meeting that didn't have to happen at that time but was an example of a colleague exercising their power over me.

I basically stuffed all this anger inside and tried to hide it away. I saw male colleagues getting angry and regularly losing their shit in meetings, but it didn't feel acceptable for women to do it. I never saw women do it. Or if they did, there was a lot of fallout afterwards.

When I headed out on my lunch break, I saw it. I also saw it after work in the nearby pubs and bars. Women who were furious. Women sat with other women and airing their grievances. Some smoked (when smoking was still a thing). Many went through a list of people they couldn't stand the sight of and wanted to kill. Others could barely touch their potato wedges (these were very fashionable for a while) because they were so incensed.

I was the same. I got angry in my lunch hour and I got angry after work. I didn't know what to do with that anger in the office.

And newsflash… a lot of the anger was directed *at other women I worked with*. This isn't surprising as we are all socially conditioned to see other women as competition. There is a feeling of scarcity when it comes to women at the top of the tree so we want to knock as many off their perches as we can. This results in anger and directing a lot of energy into slagging other women off. This is what we do on social media (maybe not in the comments but certainly when talking to our friends) and it happens at work. We haven't been provided with the tools to be direct with one another so if a female colleague does something that pisses us off, we smile, walk away and then slag them off for a good half an hour afterwards.

Glennon Doyle (one of my favourite writers and author of *Untamed: Stop Pleasing, Start Living*), has a great podcast episode[18] in which she talks about this social conditioning and how frustration at not being able to express ourselves results in anger and ultimately gossiping and negative chat. She reflects on her experience as a teacher and how boys were taught to deal with conflict versus girls:

> Every time a boy had an issue with another little boy, he would be told to deal with the other little boy in an honest and straightforward way. When the little girls had problems, the parents would be like 'be nice, be nice'.
>
> Girls were repeatedly taught to swallow their own feelings to make the other person comfortable and not cause any outer conflict. We are trained to swallow conflict and to hide it when we don't like someone, but the truth always comes out sideways. What I do believe is that women would stab each other in the back less if we when we were young we were allowed to stab each other in the front. Men are allowed to say the thing and do the thing, work through it and be direct. We have to decondition ourselves to do that.[19]

So, it's important if you're regularly feeling angry at work that you interrogate why. Is it because you are holding in some resentment about a colleague? Did you get some criticism from your boss that seemed unfair? And if this is the case then you

---

18 https://podcasts.apple.com/us/podcast/on-cussing-cattiness-what-feminism-means-to-g/id1564530722?i=1000533159734

19 Quote from *We Can Do Hard Things with Glennon Doyle,* podcast, 2021.

need to speak out rather than swallow it up and use it as fuel to bitch about it. Ultimately, slagging off colleagues doesn't get you anywhere. It doesn't change anything and it can result in a downward spiral where you start to feel increasingly disengaged with work.

It doesn't matter how much Tara Brach I listen to (another brilliant author and mindfulness guru), I still feel angry. I have found myself getting angrier, more often maybe because I have been working longer and can spot familiar patterns, in my own behaviour and in others. Some of this is also hormonal and down to sleep deprivation.

I can recognise certain personality types. I can spot a massive ego. I know when someone is just about to dump a giant turd on my desk.

And while there is greater gender equality in the office, more than there was when I first kicked off my career, a middle-aged woman getting furious is not helpful *unless* it leads to change. It's not appropriate for anyone to be angry at work (and we're thankfully beginning to see more companies get called out for their toxic, bullying work cultures).

But what do we do with the anger? What do we do if we don't want to choke on our sandwiches? What do we do with the ball of fury that sits inside? It's helpful to remember the acronym (used in addiction and recovery groups) HALT.[20] These letters stand for Hunger, Anger, Loneliness, Tiredness. They are used to help people with addictive behaviours identify whether they are about to be pushed into destructive patterns but they are also useful at work to remind ourselves to check in to see whether we are identifying our feelings correctly (i.e. we are hungry which is making us feel angry, which we are then projecting onto a colleague). So, ask yourself:

---

20 https://bradfordhealth.com/halt-hunger-anger-loneliness-tiredness

- Why do I feel this?
- Am I angry? Or am I feeling tired or hungry instead? (If you are, what can you do to address this first?)
- What can I control and what is out of my control?
- How can I phrase this issue to my boss/colleague in a direct, yet constructive way (without being apologetic or 'nice')?
- What can I address about my own behaviour to stop it from happening again? (Maybe you are complicit in this scenario and need to have a word with yourself to stop it from happening again.)

The thing is, anger is perfectly acceptable if you channel it for change. If the anger remains then listen to some angry music for a while (I was addicted to angry music for a large part of my career because I was essentially a wuss at work and let people walk all over me and so was permanently in a state of unresolved fury). Then go back into the office and address the things you've written down.

Remember that anger is valid. It is normal. It is often a sign that something needs to change.

Releasing Anger Playlist

This is music to listen to when you are feeling angry and in need of release. (You will note that they are all from a certain time period reflective of the fact that I am 48.)

- Rage Against the Machine: 'Killing In the Name'. The lyrics are great because they include a lot of swearing. This song isn't about work at all but if it helps you get through the day then that's fine.
- Hole: 'Violet'. I often ask myself, 'What would Courtney Love do in this crap situation?' and then enjoy the scenario playing out in my mind.
- Soundgarden: 'Black Hole Sun'. Just visualising the apocalypse feels strangely soothing. It puts work in its proper perspective again.
- DMX: 'X Gon Give It To Ya'. This helps if you have a big meeting coming up and are feeling tense and irritated already and need to release some of that pent-up energy beforehand.
- Public Image Ltd: 'Rise'. I sometimes get the urge to sing this when people are debating things for far too long and nobody wants to make a final decision on something.

What's on your angry playlist?

**Everyone Has Imposter Syndrome, Even the Founders of
Successful Businesses, Even Pop Stars
(But Maybe Not Dictators)**

A lot has been written about this subject – essentially, it's the feeling you get that you don't deserve the job/position you have, that you're not qualified enough and are therefore an imposter and will be dragged from your office quick smart to be replaced by someone far more capable than you.

I asked women to comment on how they experienced imposter syndrome and here's a flavour of their response and how they deal with it:

> Like lots of women, I definitely suffer from imposter syndrome. We all have an inner critic and an inner coach and the skill is to be able to control the critic and balance it out with the coach instead.

> I experience it on a regular basis, albeit thankfully not all the time. I have found out that it's pretty common and I am far from alone, so I try to keep my brain in check on the days that I question myself, and so I challenge my own thinking.

> Everyone feels imposter syndrome in some ways. I still have moments when I think someone's going to realise I shouldn't be here at all… So the bad news is that it never entirely goes away, but the good news is that you get much better at overcoming it. As one of my mentors once said to me, and I

now say to everyone I mentor: 'Imagine how much more fun and productive work would be if you put all of the energy you spend on worrying into doing the job.'

When I get that critical voice, then I try and look for evidence – in fact, sometimes I actually ask myself out loud, 'What proves that this is true?' Then I realise that the voice has no reason to be there at all because the evidence suggests I'm pretty competent!

One piece of advice I got was to write down your achievements and give yourself a boost. I've even found that doing this has led me to identifying new aims for the future because I'm acknowledging what I've done well before and can accomplish next.

A great tip from Kim Palmer, founder of the *Clementine* app, echoes this idea of looking for evidence and reminding yourself of the things you've done well: 'I've always struggled with feelings of imposter syndrome and for years while I was working, I let these feelings stop me from doing so many things with my career.'

Kim felt that imposter syndrome made her obsess about mistakes rather than seeing the positive things she was bringing to her role: 'I always focused on things that I wasn't good at versus really acknowledging all the amazing things I'd achieved and been bloody brilliant at.'

This is obviously common – many of us (women especially) beat ourselves up for failing at something but don't notice what we're doing right.

Kim continues: 'For me, the game-changer with this was to first recognise that these feelings are normal. Loads of people feel like this but you don't need to let them define you and what you do or don't do with your life.'

This is true. Pop stars. Actors. Leaders. Women who have seven children and run banks. They all feel it. And once you realise that everyone has it then it feels quite liberating. Basically, what you must do to move on is to not let it cripple you or stop you from doing things. I am writing today and am in the midst of an anxiety attack. It doesn't matter what's triggered it *but* all I can tell you is that the feelings are intense and my guts are churning. I am writing. I am writing and I am telling myself that I deserve to write and I am good enough to write. There is a voice which is telling me that I don't have qualifications to write this book. That I am not famous enough. That I don't have enough social media presence. That nobody is interested in what I have to say.

I am, however, ignoring that and writing anyway. This is part of the journey – the way to get over imposter syndrome and do the stuff anyway. Kim adds:

> I had to get a bit geeky and swot up on what imposter syndrome was and how to tackle it. The book that I always recommend reading is *The Imposter Cure* by Jessamy Hibberd. She talks about the fact that we must acknowledge, connect and celebrate all the things that we are doing well. So, I literally make lists all the time so I don't forget what's been going well and I really own the role I play in these. This has helped me so much.

So, if you want to move through imposter syndrome and not let it inhibit what you do, start off by making a list of things you've done well each week, acknowledge that everyone has the same feelings when they're working or doing anything they care about. Also realise that the voice will always be there and may be amplified when you're tired or haven't looked after yourself, and the negative chatter may be an indication that you need to work on your confidence and do whatever it is that makes you feel better.

Kim summarises this perfectly:

> When I get the negative feelings which still occur, I never ever think I'm not going to do that thing. I recognise that the little voice is there but that it's just not true, and I do almost everything. I also know that if I don't do these things it doesn't help my confidence at all. I get confidence from doing.

CHAPTER NINE

Does Freelance = Freedom and Happiness Forever?

Let me preface this by saying that when I started to really make money as a freelancer, I decided to go back into a part-time role. This was for several reasons:

- I didn't like the insecurity of never knowing whether there was another job around the corner.
- I didn't like the insecurity of chasing up invoices and not being able to rely on a steady amount of money coming in.
- I couldn't make it work in terms of childcare, so was sometimes paying more for childcare than I was making.
- I am a creature of habit in many ways.
- Working from home and the global pandemic made me feel like Catherine Deneuve in the Roman Polanski film *Repulsion* (Google it). Basically, like I was on my own, losing my mind and catastrophising – perhaps not looking as glam as Deneuve as I was often in my dressing gown and jogging bottoms.
- I also felt as if work was taking over my home because I was moderating groups and writing articles while sitting on my bed (this has changed since my mum came over and helped me clear out the shed so I am lucky enough to have wi-fi and a small desk to work at).

There are almost 2.2 million freelancers in the UK and we have the second fastest growth in terms of freelancers. Sixteen per cent of workers freelancing are mothers and 64 per cent of employers intend to outsource their work to freelancers.[21]

So clearly it works for many people and the idea of being your own boss, not answering to anyone else, can be very appealing.

I had a vision of freelancing which was a bit like my vision of parenting, before I became a parent. I imagined I would have time to a swim in the middle of the day. That I would have lots of quality time with my kids (instead of telling them to go away so I could get down to answering a potential work enquiry). I thought I would soak some lentils in the morning and then have time to make a delicious, nutritious dhal when my family came home (instead of throwing pasta pesto together yet again). I also thought I would be making a lot of money from journalism and writing, so would slowly move away from market research (which is a good earner but is punishing in terms of workload). I don't know how much money most journalists and writers earn on average. I mean, there are obviously famous ones who support themselves and their families but I was spending maybe two days pitching articles and was lucky if I made £150 every two weeks. Childcare for me was about £80 per day. So the maths didn't add up.

Freelancing isn't for everyone, whatever impression you get on Instagram

So, I guess what I'm saying is that freelancing isn't for everyone. It wasn't for me but I still like the idea of it. I know people who enjoy it. I know people who don't. I know that with small kids and needing some stable income, working in a permanent role is better for me *right now*. But things change and if you're learning

---

21 https://dontdisappoint.me.uk/resources/lifestyle/freelancing-statistics-uk

anything while you read this book I hope it's that it's important to keep evolving and changing. In fact, it can even be fun (really!)

So, I thought it would be useful to talk to someone who does make freelancing work and get her perspective.

Fiona Thomas is an author and runs successful writing courses. She says freelancing works for her because of the sheer flexibility it offers:

> I hate routines so being able to construct my own day based on my needs is a huge plus. I also suffer from depression and anxiety and have never found a traditional work environment that supported my needs, but freelancing has so much freedom that I feel like I have much more control over my mental state. I can do the things that help me maintain my mental health, like going for walks, sleeping more, getting therapy.

She found traditional workplaces too rigid and structured. This is true when you work in an office. You have to keep to someone else's schedule and sometimes you might have finished all your work for the day but have to hang about until your work day has finished. For Fiona, it was also about the flexibility to do the things she needed to do to take care of herself emotionally:

> All of those things were so much harder when I worked in a rigid work environment, not to mention the stigma of admitting you have mental health issues to your employer. So, freelancing gives me the ability to support myself and be the boss I always needed.

She says, however, that she did feel pressure to 'hustle' – this is very much the language of freelancing. This is the idea that you are either working on a project or scouting for the next project, and it can feel relentless. This is something Fiona experienced but not within her freelancing roles. Instead she associates it more with working in a permanent job:

> I felt it more when I was younger. When I graduated from university I felt this immense pressure to get a 'proper job' and appear successful. This was compounded by corporate culture which often takes advantage of young people and their enthusiasm, so I overworked myself because I was told that hustling was the only way to climb up the corporate ladder. Now that I'm self-employed I try to remind myself that I don't need to be at my desk from nine to five, I'm much more of an eleven to four kind of gal, and that's fine!

One of the things that I struggled with was the fact that I sometimes woke up worrying about the future when I was freelance. I could be in the middle of a chunky project but I was already worrying about whether the next one would go ahead and if it didn't, what I might do instead. I was often plagued by self-doubt too. Fiona experiences this as well:

> The thing is, I air it out! Talking about it always feels better, and owning my insecurities is something I'm proud of. I talk about it and that often encourages others to open up too. I feel seeing others doubting themselves reminds me that its normal, and that you can feel self-doubt and still move ahead and do the thing regardless.

Another reason that freelancing didn't work for me was that I felt isolated. This might have been amplified – no hang on, it was amplified – by the lockdowns and working from home more often but I missed having people around. I also found that sometimes I misconstrued emails and grew paranoid (going back to the Catherine Deneuve in *Repulsion* example here). I feel that when you can walk up to someone and ask them a question then you get a better steer of how they feel, what they're thinking and whether they can help.

Fiona has a different perspective:

Okay, I sometimes might miss particular people that I used to work with, but I don't miss being around people in general. I think as an introvert I much prefer working in solitude, which gives me the energy to bring my full self to out-of-hours socialising!

Her advice if you want to try freelancing is simple:

Figure out what you really enjoy doing, what you would like to work on even if no one is paying you. Because there is a lot of graft in the beginning that doesn't lead to immediate financial reward, so if you love what you do it will make that part much easier.

I also spoke to author and entrepreneur Annie Ridout about her freelance career. She feels clearly that freelancing worked for her as a parent and gave her the flexibility she needed:

I love working for myself – choosing my own hours, finding innovative ways to grow my businesses and not having to run ideas past anyone before going ahead. But I'm six years in and find it much easier to earn money now. In the early days, I was working so many hours and earning so little, that was hard. It meant when friends suggested dinner out, I'd panic, as I just didn't have the money for things like that. It took a lot of faith to keep going. If you can, though, it really pays off. Now, I have that flexibility I was dreaming of when I started out.

I was probably just about making the money I needed to pay the bills when I decided to go back into an office. But it's not always clear cut, and like all things work related, there are peaks and troughs. I had nice freelance clients and I had awful ones. I've had nice bosses in my permanent roles and awful ones. I have got to the ripe old age of 48 and now realise that much of my enjoyment of work stems from the people I work with and that I like being around people (if they're not arseholes). I also am a bit of a worrier so having a steady amount of money coming in helps manage that worrying. That is not to say that I won't go back to freelancing one day but it doesn't work for me right now (until I make millions of pounds from this book, or marry Duran Duran's John Taylor, or both).

For some, freelancing represents the change they need workwise. If you have a nagging feeling that you would work better for yourself, if you have some savings or are in a financial position where you don't need to generate a regular income for a while, then freelancing represents a way forward. The main thing to remember is that it isn't some sort of utopia – there are still up days and down days.

Make sure you have support, maybe friends who are freelancing that you can reach out to for advice, and it's also important to use all the tools in your mental health toolkit to keep your mindset as positive as possible. I found this was one of the things I struggled with – the unpredictability of freelancing often set off my anxiety which in turn made me less likely to see opportunities I could grab because I was too absorbed in my negative feelings.

Once you get past that anxiety, the world is your lobster.

Tension-Busting Tips for Dealing With a Crap Day

Some days, everything goes wrong. This happens whatever your age but I've found that as I've grown older I've been more prone to catastrophise when things don't go my way. This can make more stuff go wrong. On these kinds of day, you need to get out the toolbox. In fact, one thing to point out is that I always carry an array of stress-busting things in my workbag. I have a spray which is called Worry Not and gives me a blast of B vitamins. I have Bach Rescue Remedy to drop on my tongue. I usually have an essential oil to rub between my palms. I have water. I have a drawing of a rainbow that my daughter made for me. These are little things that I can use if I'm in the midst of a panic. Here are some other things that will help if you are feeling one step up from stressed, but one step down from crying – so that mid-level crap work feeling I guess:

- On your lunch break, listen to something that makes you laugh. This is a great way of dissolving tension and pent-up frustration. I usually turn to a podcast like Adam Buxton (I'm his number one fan) and it helps me regain perspective so I can shake off whatever it is that's bothering me.
- Think of something nice to do when you get home. Don't dwell on the kids' bedtime/mess/overwhelm and think of one thing you can do in the evening that will help you feel better. For me, this is a hot bath. It's boring but it really does help.
- Go into the toilet and cry and just get it all out.

- Go and get yourself something nice to drink. For me, this is sometimes one of those ridiculously expensive Frappuccino drinks. It is about 5000 calories and has little nutritional value but it is a treat and helps shake me out of my fug.
- Write down a list of things you feel grateful about to remind yourself of the big picture. This is just one day, not your entire life.
- Go for a run or schedule in some exercise – this really helps you get out of your head and shake off the stuff that's bothering you.

If none of the above works then simply acknowledge that you're having a tough day. Not every work day will be the same. If it's been really bad then just write the day off. There is always tomorrow. Have an early night with a good book and move on.

CHAPTER TEN

How to Build Your Confidence Up After a Career Break or Redundancy

You have lots of skills that you don't even realise you have

Confidence is a massive deal when it comes to being successful at work. We tell ourselves certain narratives and then we find that those narratives play out in real life. So, we come to a task and tell ourselves we won't be able to do it and then surprise surprise… we can't do it.

As we age, these ways of thinking about ourselves become more entrenched. We really start to believe that we can't change or learn new things. This means that if we've been out of the world of work we basically tell ourselves that we can't do anything anymore. Women who take career breaks to have children truly believe that they now have nothing to offer. That whole period of looking after little kids robs you of your identity. You become someone who solely caters to others' needs. What you often fail to realise is that at the same time, you are learning a whole host of new skills. You're building stamina, becoming more resilient, learning how to work in short, sharp bursts of time because you have a baby that's waking up in ten minutes; you're learning how to focus and stay focused under impossible odds (like three hours sleep) and all those skills are important skills at work. It's not that you will have to change a nappy at work but you will have to do the work equivalent – an unpleasant task that needs doing immediately and can't be put off and will result in quite a stink if you don't handle it right now.

The little train engine story

I always remember the children's story about a little train engine going up a hill. I think my dad used to read it to me and it stuck. There is essentially a big, long train that is asking all the other trains if it can be pulled up and over a hill. They refuse and make excuses because they can't be arsed. Then this little train engine, the smallest and least capable on paper, says, 'I think I can', and he steps forward and ends up puffing up this big hill, towing this massive train behind him and he keeps repeating the same refrain as he chugs along: 'I think I can. I think I can. I think I can.' The morale of the story is that this little train succeeds through sheer determination. (There are a couple of different versions but this is the one I remember.) The thing is that self-belief, the idea that you look in the mirror and think, *I can do this*, is super important. It is about mindset. If you tell yourself you can do something then you will find a way to do it.

Mindset is important if you're returning after a career break or looking to move into something new. It is also the time when that ageing, negative brain bants will start up in earnest and shower you in a pile of bad vibes:

You'll never pull this off, it will say at three in the morning.

You're fucking ancient, you silly old bag, it will say as you look for a new pair of trousers in Marks & Spencer.

You have stupid hair and everyone will laugh when you walk into the office, it will say as you stare into the bathroom mirror on the morning you're about to set off for your new job.

Being made redundant can feel like a real kick in the teeth

The circumstances around the redundancy may differ but when you leave a job there is often a sense of unfinished business. It can really make a dent in your confidence. If you've been in the same company for many years and then you lose that job, you also lose a big part of your identity and sense of status.

I found that when I took voluntary redundancy I then spent about two years questioning who I was. So much of my identity had been tied up with being a managing partner and being respected by (some of) my colleagues. I'd never believed that status was important to me but once it was taken away I really missed it. I also felt a lot of resentment towards the people who remained in the company. I'd not had any opportunity to get closure or feedback on the toxic culture and practices which had made working in the company so stressful. I spent a lot of time ruminating and trying to look for people to blame and then turning that blame towards myself and running through the times I'd made mistakes, the times I hadn't lived up to expectations... it went on and on. It meant that I didn't consider applying for senior positions because I no longer felt qualified to.

These feelings of failure, frustration, resentment, lack of identity and depression are all commonplace when it comes to being made redundant. I was fortunate in that I got a redundancy package which meant I could take some time away from work (not long, but it was enough for me to start generating an income as a freelancer). However, many people have to go straight out into the world of work and mask their underlying feelings. It's important to recognise the magnitude of what's happened.

I spoke to Emma Kangis, a work coach who specialises in helping women reboot their confidence.

Capture your core strengths

The time when we often need confidence the most – like starting a new job after redundancy – can be the moment when it deserts us and we feel ourselves slipping into a negative wormhole. These negative thought patterns make it incredibly hard to apply for jobs because your inner critic keeps telling you that you're worthless and a failure. There's a need to take a step back and really think about the things you are good at. Stop dwelling on the things that have gone wrong. Emma is clear on how to tackle this:

> First off, I suggest starting with looking at your strengths and achievements. Which strengths do you use on a daily basis and which come easily to you? Then, think of some strengths that you tend to use less but that will be useful in starting a new job. When we reflect on our strengths we tend to feel energised and this in turn increases our confidence.

It helps to write down all the things you have achieved during your career, the things you are proud of, and also to think through the things that you're good at. Don't dwell on the things that went wrong – you can learn from these things too but it's important in terms of confidence building to feed yourself as many positive messages as possible.

Surround yourself with people who will support you

It's also important when you're feeling vulnerable to have people around you who believe in your abilities and aren't going to point out the things that could go wrong or have gone wrong in the past. There may be friends whom you love dearly but have a tendency to worry on your behalf or remind you of the bad stuff that's happened in your career. There may also be ex-colleagues who have stayed in the company you used to work for, and you may find yourself getting lost in complaining about that company and the people who are there and going over old ground (this was a particular problem for me and it always made me feel drained afterwards – it didn't help me move forward in any way). Emma states that it is important to be being mindful of the kind of people you talk to about your new job. She continues:

> It doesn't make sense to tell people who are going to drag you back to your negative wormhole. Instead, think of the people in your network who always make you feel good about your achievements, and book in some time with them. I have a handful of these people and I lean on them heavily – even if I don't see them, I often text them when I feel a confidence wobble coming on.

Embrace a growth mindset

The fixed mindset is the rigid, reductive way of thinking that you can get stuck in sometimes and means you keep giving yourself the same negative claptrap. It also means that you keep rehashing what went wrong in previous roles and jobs and doesn't allow you to embrace change. Emma says we need to sit up and acknowledge when we're doing this:

> Recognise when you stray into a fixed mindset – for example, when negative stories enter your mind such as, 'I can't do this' or, 'I'm not experienced enough' – and check to see whether these stories are true. Lean into more of a growth mindset, reminding yourself of your strengths, skills, experience and positive attributes.

Quite often there is little evidence to support your negative thinking – it might be one mistake you made years ago or something a boss said to you and you really took to heart.

Reframe what you've learned while you've been away

As mentioned in Chapter Four about anxiety and work, many women feel under-confident coming back off maternity leave because they find it hard to explain the benefit of this time to a potential employer. Emma elaborates:

> Some women who have had time off work to have children don't take time to think about what their 'job' has been and the skills they have acquired during this period of absence. We are constantly learning in different ways.

It is important to acknowledge that while parenting isn't a conventional job, it is a job and requires a whole gamut of skills. It also means you're resilient and are used to having to get stuff done in a limited amount of time (if you've ever tried to get a toddler's socks and shoes on in under a minute because you're running late and must get out the door then you know what I mean). Emma says it's important to think about this parenting time as contributing to your work skills rather than a blank slate:

> Reflect on what you have been doing during this period and notice any positive, new learned behaviours and skills. You might be more organised and efficient, and it's worth acknowledging and celebrating these newly acquired skills. Talk about these desirable skills and own your experiences.

She also advises getting a mentor so you have a sounding board and someone who can give you advice and support – ideally someone who has also been away from work on maternity leave:

> Seek a mentor, perhaps someone who is working in the same field as you would like to and ideally someone who has gone back to work after a career break or having a baby. They will be able to tell you about their experience and share some insights into how they may have explained their absence from work.

Emma also has great advice for how to create an impression in your role (whether you're new or are returning after a break):

> Think about your personal brand and how you want to be perceived. This is a great opportunity to think about what has previously worked for you in your last role and what you would like to bring to the new role. Build great relationships from the start. Recognise who your stakeholders are. Remain curious and empathetic. It's tempting to arrange lots of introductory meetings within the first couple of weeks but spread these out so that you can gain a bit more perspective on the company and your peers.

Confidence is also linked to the ability to say what you do and don't want to do at work. If you don't feel confident then you're more likely to agree to working longer hours or to taking on more than you can manage. It's hard to be assertive if it's something you're unused to and as women we often feel apologetic for saying what we want and need. It's important, Emma says, to stick to your guns:

> If working part time, you don't want to be working five days in four! Avoid saying yes to everything, especially if you know you may not be able to deliver. There might be times when you

are unavailable due to other commitments such as childcare, so create effective work/non-work boundaries from the onset and make sure you are putting these boundaries in to practice!

Alice Olins, founder of the Step Up Club, which helps women to 'overcome work challenges and take their careers to new heights', has this advice in terms of building confidence:

Build your confidence by seeing yourself taking on challenges. A lot of our confidence rests in our inner voice and there's often a lot of work that can be done around how we view ourselves; confidence also develops by recognising when we step out of our comfort zone. Challenging ourselves builds self-efficacy, a subset of confidence, and when these risks pay off, the rewards continue to fuel this positive confidence fire. When they go awry, we also grow because we realise we are stronger than we perhaps thought, and there are always so many lessons and much learning when things don't go your way. Try it and you will win, whatever the outcome.

CHAPTER ELEVEN

What Kind of Brand Are You? How to Harness Your Uniqueness More Effectively

Is it wanky to consider yourself a brand?

Yes, yes it is, but it's also quite useful because it allows you to get more of an objective steer on your work persona.

I remember when someone first told me to think of myself as a brand I thought how pretentious that sounded. *A brand?* The thing is that nowadays, what with this thing called social media that we're all addicted to, and so much of our identities living online, it's likely that employers and potential employers and colleagues will have certain perceptions of you before you even come in for an interview.

They might have looked at your LinkedIn profile or have seen your Instagram account. So how do you harness these platforms so that they help rather than hinder? If I Google myself right now, I find a whole host of images and blogs I've written and many of them are helpful and not helpful. If I wanted to go into banking then potentially not helpful but as I have a career as a writer and working in social media, it's more helpful. I have co-written a book about orgasms and sex. I've also written articles about liking wild swimming and celebrating not being married. On my Instagram, the story is worse with a lot of badly made reels of me doing push-ups in the bedroom and trying to do the running man (for a while

I believed this would produce a meaningful income but I now know that the life of an influencer is tough and it's dog-eat-dog, and you must be on your phone even more than I am right now, which would mean I wouldn't look up at all).

However, it seems that others view me entirely differently. An interesting exercise is to ask friends to describe you – this can help you get an understanding (without the inner critic feeding you bad vibes) of what your brand is all about.

Spend a few minutes thinking what words your friends would use and how these words/skills could be applied to positioning yourself in an interview or on LinkedIn. For a long time, our personal sides were locked away and we were expected to put on a professional front that perhaps didn't resemble our core personality at all. That has now (thankfully) changed, so you should feel you have a synergy between the person you are at home and the person you are at work (at home you may be messier and swear more). If there is a massive disparity between who you are in both spheres then that can feel exhausting and it's worth thinking about how to be more authentic so you don't feel as if you must perform at work all the time. (I have been hopeless at this in the past and often end up telling colleagues my life story. This isn't ideal either – you need some sort of boundary in place.)

I spoke to Alice Olins about branding and how to be more single-minded and thoughtful in the way you're positioning yourself online. Alice believes that social media offers a big opportunity:

> The aim of developing and sharing a personal brand is to become more memorable, to strengthen your voice within your industry – and potentially beyond – and to be able to create new opportunities for yourself.

Alice feels that social media is incredibly useful for networking. Whereas before you might have gone to a conference and stood awkwardly with a stale cheese sandwich and a glass of white wine, now you can gain access to all sorts of people who can be helpful in building your career or helping you change direction.

> Brand building is closely aligned to growing and nurturing your network and so it's also important to be active on several professional or social platforms, because they allow you to connect to others in ways and with the ease and speed that means there really are no boundaries anymore in terms of who we connect to and what we can create for ourselves.

Some of us (say those who have written books about orgasms) can feel that there is a bit of a mix of personal/professional content out there if people Google us. Alice doesn't see this as a problem (within reason); she elaborates on this:

> The main point here is authenticity. I don't think there is such a thing as over-sharing if that is your way of communicating and it's what your followers and community know and love you for. Obviously, in more professional circumstances it's important to respect your organisation because as an employee, you are representing *their* brand and we must take that seriously and treat it with sensitivity. That said, I am a huge advocate of bringing your whole self to your workspace. Sharing stories about your life, your family, your passions is how you create deep, lasting and career-defining relationships with others, and we must not be fearful of showing who we really are. In short, we need to be able to show our full selves so that we can feel comfortable being vulnerable; when we can connect to others with truth and transparency it allows for a sense of belonging within teams and across collaborators that gives us

the freedom and power to deliver bad news, test new waters, share our needs and allow for out-of-the-box thinking.

And finally, what about our CV? How do we brand ourselves on there?

Alice believes that your CV needs to be a piece of engaging content in its own right. All too often we are tied to a rigid template whereas now it needs to keep a potential employer's attention. This doesn't mean sticking funny collages all over it but it's more about editing it so that your brand comes to the fore and someone who has never met you before 'gets' a strong sense of what skills you can bring.

Alice provides more detail on this:

> I think for many employed women CVs are still very impor-tant. Many that I see need modernising, both visually and in terms of how we tell our story. My top tip: your bio is key, so make sure you tell a compelling story. Think about the *feeling* that your story creates in others; like a novel, give it a beginning a middle and an end – include a high, a low that you overcame and add in specific examples.

So, remember that you want someone to feel enthusiastic and energised by your CV. Don't make it a long list of stuff. Don't bother telling them that you like swimming. Be braggy about your achievements.

Interview Tips:
How to Make People Want to Work With You

Interviews are another murky area to navigate and as you grow older you may start to feel weary at the thought of them. There is tons of advice out there on how to 'nail that interview' (hate that phrase) but here's some of my own tips based on my experience of interviewing loads of people.

I have interviewed a lot of people. In my previous job, the one where I stayed too long, I would interview two or three people a week, and I firmly believe that each time my instincts about the person I was interviewing turned out to be right. There are some common misconceptions when people are interviewed; one of them is the belief that they need to use the time to prove to the interviewer that they are cleverer than everyone else out there.

I sat through many interviews where people were so clever and wanged on about how clever they were but I could tell by their lack of humility that they would be a nightmare to work with, that they'd find it hard to collaborate or help others learn and that ultimately, they'd not get through projects without a lot of crap happening along the way. I am not saying that having the right skills isn't important, but not as crucial as having empathy, being able to collaborate with others and being positive about problem-solving.

Essentially, when someone is interviewing you, they are trying to imagine what it will be like working with you day to day. Will you be someone who immediately flags up the things that have gone wrong and all the challenges ahead?

Here are some straightforward interview tips to ensure you're showcasing yourself in the best light possible:

- Always make sure you know exactly where you're going and how long it'll take to get there. It sounds obvious but running late because you haven't researched the location properly makes you feel stressed and overwhelmed before the interview has even started. Try and arrive about 30 minutes before and grab a coffee nearby so you can rehearse some of your answers and can turn up calm and composed.

- Make sure you research the company properly so you know lots of background about them and their values. Make sure your values align with theirs. That way, when you're describing yourself you can drop in lots of ways that your skills and values have a natural synergy with theirs.

- Smile as much as you can but not so much that it's creepy. This is particularly true on Zoom interviews because we have a tendency to just stare into our laptops as if our souls are being zapped out through our eyeballs.

- Think about your clothing and the company you want to work for. Look at some of the LinkedIn profiles of their staff. I hate to say it but decisions are often made on how we present ourselves visually and style comes into that. If it's a creative job then you can afford to push the envelope but the most important thing is that you feel comfortable and confident. Be yourself but don't rock up in jeans, grubby trainers and a smear of toothpaste on your chin. The important thing is that you've made an effort.

- It's always good to have a few questions of your own at the end of the interview just to show that you're enthusiastic about the role and not just going through the motions.

- Keep answers short and don't go off on wild tangents or talk about too much personal stuff (this is a biggie with me as I tend to overshare things that are unnecessary and not relevant to the question I've been asked).

- Be honest about yourself. It can feel scary and vulnerable but it also demonstrates that you know your own values and are confident talking about them.

- Choose some achievements that fit with the role you're applying for. Think of concrete examples of ways you've helped the people you worked for achieve their objectives, such as, 'I increased their social media following by 30 per cent.' Show that if they hire you they are likely to see the same or even better results.

- Acknowledge that you're nervous and if you make a mistake when you're talking, just apologise and pick up your strand of thought again. It's much easier to say, 'Gosh I was rambling there because I'm nervous', and acknowledge what's happening than pretend everything is normal.

- Loads of interviews are done over video call now. This is hard as it's difficult to gauge the interviewer or how the interview is going and there can be a tendency for the whole tone to be quite flat and unemotional. On a practical level, make sure you're not going to be interrupted by children/pets/noise and also that your connection is okay. Think about your background. I recently did an interview in my bed and it was only afterwards I realised it didn't look professional because I had hand cream and the book I was reading next to my head. Try and sit at a desk and if you can artfully arrange some clever looking/relevant books behind you then there's no harm in that.

- Breathe. This is really important. When we're nervous we have a tendency to forget to breathe deeply and this can mean our words come out in a slightly out-of-breath, incoherent way but also our nervous feelings are amplified. Don't be afraid to pause and just breathe for a couple of seconds. This will slow you down and help settle your nerves.

- Remember that these are just people you're talking to. They are trying to visualise what it will be like working with you so give them a good impression and the sense that you're a safe pair of hands.

Fashion Tips for Your Forties (Or What to Wear to the Office When Nobody Cares Anymore)

One of the best things that has happened in modern work culture is the fact that many industries no longer have a strict dress code. If you're a lawyer or work in finance then you are probably expected to wear a suit but for many offices you can get away with wearing pretty much what you like.

Having said that, I like to dress up for the office. This doesn't mean that I wear a suit but it does mean that I make more of an effort than the days that I'm working from home. I enjoy fashion and throughout my career I have often thought through what I was going to wear the next day and planned it out. Wearing clothing that makes you feel good is really helpful when it comes to work. It makes you feel more confident, competent and pulled together.

It sounds daft but I've found that clothing is often an icebreaker at work. I have spent a lot of my career complimenting people on their clothes. It's the first thing we see when we meet a person and there isn't anyone I've come across who doesn't enjoy being told their shirt/shoes/scarf are really nice.

There aren't any rules with fashion but nonetheless I spoke to fashion blogger Kate Hiscox to see if she had any advice for office-wear. She says:

I never worked in an office that had a dress code. If I ever wore a blazer to work people would ask me if I was going for a job interview! I always had standards though. No flip-flops, no short shorts, nothing that I would feasibly wear on a beach, that kind of thing.

Kate does believe that having a few good basics is helpful if you're returning to work after a break:

I don't think women should try and dress 'young' though, just to fit in. That will just come across as trying too hard. You just have to dress as yourself, but maybe a more dressed-up version of yourself. I'd go for classic basics if I was returning to the office: a good dress, well-cut trousers, a good shirt and shoes. Shoes are always my most important thing. No scruffy trainers. I'd go for classic white trainers, loafers, or boots in the winter.

Hair and make-up

On a personal level, I have found that hair is important. I used to think that all successful women had bobs and that somewhere there was a tablet with the words 'Boss hair rules', and on there would be the inscription 'ALL BOSSES MUST HAVE BOBS' emblazoned across the top. In fact, if you look at the covers of *Time* magazine at the female bosses who have made the cover, I would say that 90 per cent have bobs. The message seems to be that women with bobs are serious at business whereas women with long hair are not.

I say bollocks to it and wear your hair as you like and don't let anyone tell you otherwise.

Crying in the Toilet and
Why It's Actually a Good Thing at Work

This diagram effectively brings to life how much time I have spent working versus crying. I can honestly say, however, that if I hadn't done the crying then I wouldn't have done any of the work at all.

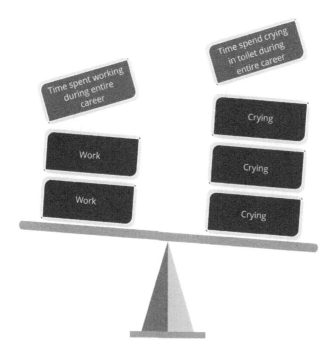

I have done a lot of crying in toilets. When I was going through fertility treatment there were times when I had to take my drugs into work and would receive a phone call and would have go into the work toilet and inject myself in my tummy because I was going through the stimulating phase of my IVF cycle.

The drugs themselves would make me cry but then the surrealness of the situation (getting a hypodermic needle out of its plastic cover and trying to pretend I was just rummaging around for a tampon) itself would make me feel even worse.

I once took a pregnancy test in a viewing facility toilet just before I had to moderate a group and then cried because it was negative (you take a lot of pregnancy tests when you're trying for a baby and sometimes I would do a double bluff and take them at work because I thought it would be positive, just because it was such an odd place to take a pregnancy test (your mind does weird things when you're desperate to have a child).

Parking this fertility stuff, there were also a lot of times when I came out of long, tiresome board meetings, meetings where I'd been ignored or criticized, or meetings where I'd felt I'd said something daft or nothing at all, and then I'd head straight for the toilet, put the seat down, flush the chain, so nobody could hear me, and have a good weep.

I have wept a lot in work toilets. After bad appraisals. After appraisals where there was one piece of criticism but I focused just on that one bit and let it dominate everything else. I have cried and I have also given myself pep talks. The two kind of go hand in hand.

Crying in front of colleagues is okay if that's your thing but for me, well I like to preserve a bit of myself, and unless I'm really upset (like the time I sat in a board meeting and burst into tears because I'd just suffered a miscarriage and thought I was okay but I wasn't) then I think crying in the toilet is no bad thing.

You can cry. You can vent the feelings. If you need to you can make a plan of attack – this is where the pep talk comes in and you say to yourself that you're going to be okay but also decide what you're going to do next. Then when you need to talk to your boss or whomever it is (if it's work-related crying and not just life fatigue), you can talk in a calm and more ordered way.

It has taken me a long time (more than 30-odd years) to realise that crying is normal. It is also quite likely to happen at work because we spend so much time there. Crying in toilets works for me because it means I can do it in private and collect my thoughts before tackling the underlying causes. I've found that crying in front of colleagues isn't very helpful. It also (unfortunately) makes some male colleagues think they were right all along and that women can't navigate the challenges of work as well as men.

So, if you're having a crap day, don't feel ashamed. Get the seat down. Flush the chain.

Cry and then ready yourself for your return to the work fray.

The Pivot – How Do You Do It?

If you look it up online then you'll see that pivot means to turn on, or as if on, a pivot. It is also a buzz word and seems to have come into fashion a bit like the 'side hustle' which is now old hat. In my last book, I said 'side hustle' was basically 'hobbie' unless it was a business in which case, why not call it 'my business'.

Anyway, the idea of a pivot is very appealing as it implies that you can basically jack in your old job and do an about turn. For example, from marketing executive to trapeze artist. Or lion tamer to turkey farmer. I don't have any problem with the word itself and think that by the time you get to your forties you really need to have decided or be in the process of deciding whether you're in the right line of work or whether you need to try something new. The something new is going to be shaped by lots of factors, though, like whether you can afford to give up your job, whether you have to retrain, whether you're just getting a case of 'the grass is greener', which can often happen when you've been in the same job for a long time.

If the pivot works, however (and if you research what you want to do next, and have a plan in place in case it goes wrong), then it can inject new energy into your professional life. I love reading stories of people who have switched jobs in their forties and fifties and finally hit on something they like much more. I recently realised that I myself have pivoted but hadn't really seen it as such. I started in fast-food, I went into furniture retail, then market research, then blogging, then writing, then social media management, then market research and am now doing a combination of different things.

I spoke to Kate Hiscox, who worked in the record industry for many years and recently decided to go it alone. It wasn't an overnight process – she'd been steadily building up her fashion blogging brand and growing her followers on Instagram (she is @wearsmymoney and is brilliant at recommending clothes that work for women in their forties that are on trend and wearable).

One of the things she enjoys about her pivot is the benefits it has offered her compared with working in her old role in the record company. Kate says:

> I'm really loving the freedom I now have working for myself. I can decide how much I do and when I do it. I often work in the evenings so I don't have to do so much in the day if I've got other things I want to do. Not something I could have done working for a company.

Kate also knew that the record industry wasn't particularly welcoming to older women and so it had made her feel insecure and on the back foot in terms of what the future might hold:

> I didn't mean to change careers, but I did know I wanted a way out of my job in the music business as it's really not kind to women over 45. The constant threat of redundancy isn't pleasant.

A successful pivot is not suddenly throwing caution to the wind and resigning from your job and telling everyone you work with that they suck (well, you can do that but you may regret it later). A successful pivot is preparing your move in advance so that you feel secure and the role you're moving into feels watertight. By *watertight* I mean that you're confident you can do it, or at least 50 per cent of it, the company/work makes you feel good, and the role is as secure as it can be. An example of this would be when I moved from market research agency work to become a blog editor. I'd been doing this on the side because I loved writing and reading about parenting challenges (this was for the Selfish Mother blog). I knew that I had enough savings to survive and could combine editing with freelance market research. The role wasn't that secure, but by the time I stopped doing it, I had a steady enough income from freelancing.

One of the things to be mindful of is not leaping into a new role just because you really detest your current one. This is like jumping from one bad relationship into the next. It is just a different kind of bad (and I've done this – chiefly because of the financial pressure I've felt at the time – but when I've done it, it's never worked out, and I've soon been looking for a new role again).

Going back to Kate and her pivot. First off, she'd already got an established brand through writing her fashion blog and she finally made the move to doing this full time and being a consultant:

> I started writing the blog as a hobby as I always wanted to write and I love fashion. I didn't start making any real money until more recently. That's when I realised I could sustain myself without having a salaried job. I don't necessarily have the same income, but I have so much more freedom and that counts for more these days for me.

So, here's how to execute an excellent pivot:

- Start planning and researching before you make the leap.
- Think about what you want from your next move – what are the most important criteria – more autonomy? Or more creativity?
- Talk to women who have pivoted already and ask them for advice.

- Don't always believe that the grass is greener – you may earn less money or face other challenges, and there is no such thing as the perfect job.

CHAPTER TWELVE

Female Bosses: Why They Should Lift as They Climb (But Not All Do)

In my survey, it was clear that bosses weren't always particularly inspiring. Of the women I spoke to, 47.5 per cent said that friends were more inspiring in terms of work goals, and 30 per cent claimed that there simply weren't any women out there who inspired them. Depressingly, nobody said that they found themselves inspiring (which is why I wrote this book, or is part of the reason because I am always meeting inspiring women, and then realizing that they don't find themselves inspiring when they seriously are).

I've had a mixed experience with female bosses. I would love to tell you that I have had punchy, gutsy, empathetic, confident, honest and authentic women who have managed me well throughout my entire career but the truth is that if that had been the case then I probably wouldn't have written this book and would have simply been gliding along through my work life with no doubt, crippling anxiety or overwhelm (though much of this has been self-inflicted and part of the broader patriarchy which tells women they are flops and failures all their lives). I have had a couple of female bosses who were downright evil and could have given Cruella de Vil a run for her money, and a couple who seemed okay but when push came to shove, they reverted to the male status quo. One boss I had seemed to be such a shape shifter that I felt utterly disorientated – one minute a feminist (in female company), the next a complete sexist bastard (as soon as an alpha male walked into the room). I shouldn't even talk about Cruella in this paragraph because I'm simply using the same lazy stereotypes that the media and broader culture rely on when depicting female bosses.

Female bosses that we see in films or in the right-wing media (who often like to rely on old stereotypes) are usually very samey and typically:

- are cold, masculine and competitive
- wear their hair bobbed (this was something I noticed when I started moving in the influencer world too – they also seemed to have bobbed hair. Was this a strange conspiracy? Were bobbed women programmed to take over the world?)
- wear shoulder pads
- have zero humour
- are hard to get on with
- are workaholics
- ignore mothers or the fact that they are mothers
- are no fun.

The following diagram brings to life how a certain style of female boss kept being replicated again and again. I saw it in the organisation that I worked in. Women would come in with excellent work skills – things like being empathetic, being creative, being open minded, being collaborative. They would then see that the kind of women who tended to be at the top were hard, had no people skills and were hierarchical and domineering and so they would mirror these characteristics to get ahead. Ultimately, the culture, the predominantly masculine culture, created a whole agency of women who were fucking awful to work with.

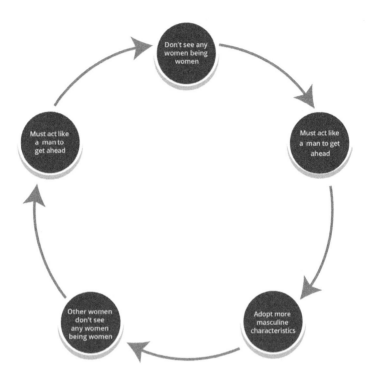

Now we are starting to see a more diverse set of female leaders emerging. We still have massive issues with diversity in terms of race. And we have issues around women who are mothers being in senior positions. But we are starting to realise that the more feminine attributes like empathy are powerful in the workplace. This is an exciting time because it feels as if women are being seen in a different light when it comes to leadership and don't have to adopt male characteristic to succeed. There is still a lot of work to be done, though, as I've touched on before. There aren't enough realistic and relatable images of female leaders. There are not enough conversations about what happens when these leaders have children. Or when these leaders choose not to have children. There are not enough conversations about what happens when these leaders go through the menopause. Or infertility. We gain comfort through hearing these narratives because we realise that we're not alone. We also realise that being a leader isn't something 'only a certain type of women can do'. If we see women we relate to, then we believe we can do it too.

There are two key issues for me now that I'm in my late forties:

1. I want my daughters to see women at the top who inspire them and I want these women to be diverse and not all cut from the same cloth.
2. I don't myself want to be a boss. I am too tired. This is not a failure or a signal that I lack ambition. I just don't want it.

This is a hard one as I know others must look at me and wonder why I don't want to be a boss. It's because our career paths have always been depicted as climbing vertically and haven't been about stepping off the ladder or climbing up a different one entirely.

It's also hard because I still want to be paid what I'm worth (so even if I'm taking on fewer leader/boss responsibilities I think I should be paid for my years of experience and the skills I've collected over those years).

I don't mind being managed by someone younger than me. I know that I don't want the hours that a boss must commit to. I don't want the late-night emails. I don't want the shit. I have been there and have experienced it first-hand. I had the bob FFS! I had shares in Whistles blazers and I can tell you that aside from the financial rewards there was little to recommend being a boss.

I am now at the stage that I wave the younger women through. I stand in my mid-level position and say, *'You go, you young women. You charge ahead. Full of energy and full of verve. Watch me lie on the floor here and watch* Too Hot to Handle *on Netflix while you do another Zoom meeting. You take it. It is yours. I hand the mantle to you all.'*

So, the issue of bosses for me is more about not being total bitches when they're managing me and ensuring that there is enough diversity in terms of the types of women represented at the top table so that younger women can see women who inspire them. And not just younger women, also older women who still aspire to be bosses, because they can be bosses too.

As part of my investigation into female bosses, I interviewed some senior women anonymously – these women worked in marketing, branding and consultancy agencies and I was interested to find out what their experiences were like.

One woman talked about how much energy and empathy a female boss had put into her role to the point where she had no balance herself:

> I had an amazing boss for a couple of years. She had set up her own agency because her role in a big ad agency was incompatible with having small kids. She hired women, she managed a roster of senior freelance planners who had quit full-time roles for the same reasons she did. She gave women great work opportunities and the scope to balance this work with their family lives. The thing that really bothers me is that this brilliant (sometimes difficult) boss never got a healthy balance in her life. Nothing approaching it. And just as she thought she was there, she was diagnosed with cancer and she died a year later. One of the defining lines I remember from her memorial was that she 'cared' – she cared about her employees and her planner network (it was a funny sort of family), she cared so deeply about her work. She cared probably too much, too often.

Another woman who used to work in advertising at a senior level said:

It's interesting that when I reflect on my own female bosses there were certainly examples where they could not switch off and were so driven and preoccupied by work that not only did it not hold up a good example to other women (or anyone for that matter), it also took a toll on their decision-making and mental health. So my boss would lose her temper and get frustrated because people weren't putting the same amount of energy into their work as she was.

Sometimes our own high (perfectionist) expectations of ourselves mean that the vibes we're sending out to others are that work is something that should always be prioritised at the expense of everything else. I have also noticed that women I've worked with struggle more with helping to set boundaries and so will email on non-work days, early in the morning and late at night. Often when you look under the surface you realise that their own boundaries are all over the place so they are setting an example that as a woman you are essentially expected to be always available to reply to queries, always online, never off.

To be a good female boss basically means looking at the way you want to be managed and setting the example. Working with boundaries. Being empathetic. Being critical but in a constructive way and having a growth mindset and learning from others (not rigid and stuck in your ways). Increasingly, it's also about offering flexibility and, if you're a parent, thinking about what kind of set-up works best for those of your employees who are parents too.

The workaholic female boss

When I've observed female bosses up close I've realised that they are often the ones who are working harder than anyone else in the company. They have something to prove and a couple of them have worked so hard that they've basically had nervous breakdowns.

It's also incredibly hard to be a good leader when you're so worn down and tired yourself that you are close to crying. It also means you tend to blow up the minute something goes wrong. I had one female boss who constantly lost her temper, bullied people and dominated meetings – essentially everyone in the company was scared to sit near her or say anything in case she 'went off'. Now with the benefit of hindsight I can see she was trying to navigate three young children, a global company and high business targets. She had a lot to prove and believed that a heavy workload was the only way to do it. This became the work ethic for the entire company because people were hired who were also workaholics and made work their highest priority. So, the entire culture of the company became toxic because nobody was prioritising their well-being and everyone was working too hard. This can happen for a good while but eventually people leave, or are signed off, or have breakdowns and then projects go off the rails and ultimately it all goes wrong.

It feels now that there are more positive female role models who are bosses but nonetheless there are still a lot of martyrs/workaholics out there, women who don't prioritise their health and well-being (and send out the message that work is more important than anything else) and women who are too rigid in the way that they manage their workforce. The other thing I've seen a lot is how some women are completely different when they're in 'boss mode' compared with when they're relaxed and in their more personal mode. This makes them come across as inauthentic and weird.

Ultimately, you can have an awful male boss or an awful female boss – it's more about your values. In my survey, the key characteristics that came forward as important when being managed were:

- empathy (40 per cent of women believed this was important)
- authenticity (45 per cent thought this was a priority).

Funnily enough, many of us have worries that we are not intellectual enough in the workplace but 5 per cent thought 'being clever' was important for senior women, while humour emerged as just as important (I'm not saying that you can be funny and stupid but more that humour is an important skill when you're managing people – it can help diffuse tension, and laughter releases endorphins which help us navigate stressful situations).

Top five women I would like to be my boss

Michelle Obama
Sharon Horgan
Glennon Doyle
Dawn French
Oprah Winfrey

When I look at the women who would be my fantasy bosses I realise that they all share certain qualities. They are funny. They are authentic. They are empaths. They are also (I imagine) not scared to give direction. They are creative. They (and I don't know them personally but in my imagination) are strong. They also acknowledge how leadership can be challenging at times.

Women bosses don't need to be meek and mild. They don't need to be liked all the time but they do need to have some of the above qualities.

Get the Thing You Hate Done First – or 'Eating the Frog'

In each and every work day there is a task or tasks that you know will be difficult or will require a lot of concentration or may be quite the opposite and mind-numbingly boring. In these situations, the best tactic is to do that thing first thing before you do anything else.

Do you remember when you were at school and you had to do some homework and instead of doing it you let it hang over you all weekend and then it got to Sunday night and you were already full of dread about Monday morning being on its way but you also had this shitty piece of homework that had to be done but now you were practically immobolised at the thought of starting it because it had been lurking too long in your periphery and you should have just done it already?

Mark Twain once said: 'If it's your job to eat a frog then it's best to do it first thing in the morning. And if it's your job to eat two frogs, it's best to eat the biggest one first,' meaning that it's best to just *do it* and get it over with without procrastinating.

This is also true when you're looking for jobs and hate LinkedIn or can't be bothered to tackle your out-of-date CV or reach out to the person you know could help you. Sit down. Identify the most important task you have been putting off. Or the thing that will be hardest to do so you're dreading it. Do it. Keep doing this each day.

CHAPTER THIRTEEN

Five Secrets of the Female Yodas of This World

Sometimes I like to imagine this scenario: I am on my deathbed. Ryan Gosling and some other Hollywood heartthrobs are crying at my feet (but they are not the same age as me – they have remained young for some reason and are hopelessly in love with me even though I look like a well-aged woman, whatever that means).

My children are also with me and they have grown up to be amazing, beautiful, confident women. They are single-handedly redesigning housing so it is more ecologically friendly or they are in the process of becoming the first female astronaut from the UK to land on the moon and my partner is there too and he is looking a bit jealous because of the Hollywood actors being in love with me but is also very much in love with me so understands where they're coming from.

I digress.

There is a young female colleague who is seated next to my bed and she has a notepad in her hand and a pen poised over this notepad.

'What is it you want to know?' I whisper to her as she stares earnestly into my eyes.

She reaches forward and strokes my arm – a gesture that doesn't feel weird as I'm dying and it's the kind of thing you do to make someone feel a bit better about the fact that they're about to disappear forever.

'I want to know the secret of being happy and successful at work,' she says.

'She has no idea,' my partner says and I slap his hand because I still have enough strength to do that despite being on my last legs.

'I do. I know exactly what the secret is. Lean closer and I'll tell you.'

The young woman leans forward and I whisper in her ear.

She nods enthusiastically. She doesn't need to write it down because I've been short and to the point. And what did I say? What one piece of advice did I give this woman in my imaginary scenario with actors at my feet and my successful children (by their own definition – forget becoming astronauts or anything else).

Well, that's the problem. In my ideal fantasy, I would say, 'Don't eat shit for anyone.'

Or perhaps even, 'Don't let anyone make you feel bad.'

But I would probably say, 'Remember that work is not everything. It matters but it also doesn't matter. Now that I'm here, now that I've only got a few moments left… well, that's what I've realised.'

And then I'd pass into the great unknown and I sincerely hope that there'd be no offices up there with whirring printers and air con, or bean bags designed to give the illusion of freedom and creativity but are, in reality, impossible to get up from, and there'd be no Friday beers or ping pong tables or meetings that went on for four hours with nothing resolved or men with booming voices yawning on about Baudelaire and his impact on the semiotics of dry shampoo. I'd leap into the clouds and finally, finally, my work would be done.

If you found none of the above entirely helpful, I've listed below some excellent work advice for women in their forties and beyond from some of the experts I spoke to writing this book.

Kim Palmer, founder of the *Clementine* app:

Get nerdy. Sit down and take a helicopter view of your work life and work out 1) what's working (because we often forget there is plenty of good stuff) and then 2) what's not working. Then create an action plan to change some of the things that aren't working. Sounds simple but you really do need to sit down, reflect and work through this stuff.

Sarah Tomczak, editor of *Red* magazine:

Just as Dolly Parton says, 'Don't get so busy making a living that you forget to make a life'. It's likely that we will be working for at least another 30 years, so it's vital to create flexibility that allows you to enjoy your life (kids/relationship/travel/health) alongside your career.

Helen Serafinowicz, writer of cult TV series *Motherland*:

I juggle so many aspects of my life so with a deadline I don't focus on the in-between worky bit. I just cross my fingers and think by this date I will have done it. And if I haven't then I tell myself nobody's going to die (and nine times out of ten nobody has ever died).

Annie Ridout, author and founder of *The Robora*, an online course platform:

First, work on your confidence. When you feel confident, amazing things can happen. Doors open, you start to try out new ideas without letting fear hold you back, and you worry less about what people will think. So, I'd recommend coaching, or joining an online course or group programme that helps you to build confidence.

Emma Kangis, life coach:

Own your identities (work/parent/career/friend…) and recognise what makes you feel confident when acquiring these identities. We are often tired, trying to juggle and fulfil obligations at work and be there for our families. Getting the balance right can be tricky, but it is doable. Align your personal and professional life with your values. The happier we are, the more confident we feel.

Anna Whitehouse, campaigner, author and broadcaster:

My advice is to physically write to-do lists instead of putting them in notes. Way more satisfying to cross off too.

Hilda Burke, psychotherapist, life coach and couples' counsellor:

I have many women who come to see me aged 40–55 who are questioning their careers. Perhaps they've achieved what they consider the 'pinnacle' of their career path but haven't received what they expected. The work with them involves looking at their conditioning, what's been put onto them in terms of expectations by others (which in time have become their own expectations) and peeling back the layers to find out who they really are. That might manifest in many different shapes: their friendships, relationships, interests but often it's in their careers as well. This work doesn't happen overnight but it really merits addressing those internal niggly questions such as, 'Why am I doing this?' and, 'What's the point to my work?'

Jo Wimble-Groves, tech entrepreneur, author and founder of Guilty Mother blog:

My advice is to embrace your whole self – your strengths, your flaws, your weaknesses – and commit to spending the next 40 years growing and developing your best self. In my view, we spend a lot of time in our twenties and thirties battling our inner critic, worrying about our weight and other people's opinions of us. My hope for girls and women is that by we time we hit the magic number 40, we finally find ways to silence that inner critic or the critics that surround us. There's a question I often get asked on interviews and podcasts which is, if you could speak to your 20-year-old self, what would you say? It's such a thought-provoking way of encouraging you to remember how far you have come.

Alice Olins, founder of the Step Up Club:

I suppose my top pieces of advice are around finding the power and control to live the professional lives that feel right at the time. By that I mean, our definition of success evolves as we do, and it's important that we check in with ourselves, to make sure our needs are being met, that are values are being respected and that we're feeling fulfilled and inspired. With the general overwhelm and burnout that's around, I find that a lot of women stick in jobs that are okay, but not right, because it feels easier to not rock the boat. I think this type of fearful, short-term thinking does more damage. Change is hard, and a lot of my work is around helping women to realise that change is positive and exciting; we have more control than we tend to think over our professional destiny, but we must find the courage to be able to leap when we're coasting. Also, leaning on others, it's vital, and there's no shame in that.

Dr Becky Quicke, psychologist specialising in perimenopause and menopause:

Perimenopause strengthens our inner bullshit detectors, especially within the workplace, and we just can't tolerate it anymore! I would encourage you to own this as a midlife strength and call it out rather than letting the frustration and anger eat away inside you.

Flic Taylor, journalist, writer and broadcaster:

Gone are the days of trying to please, overwork, and achieve on an outstanding level every day. Please don't wear a busyness badge of honour, like I did. If you've got one pinned to your jacket, take it off right now. Busy does not equal brilliant. I've learned this the hard way. Looking back, I wish I had stood up for myself at work. I wish I'd said 'no' to more things and unapologetically stated what tasks were sustainable and what tasks were not.

Clemmie Telford, writer and consultant:

Trust your instinct. I believe it's our superpower. So often the opportunities that don't feel right from the off turn out to be problematic in the long run. Same in reverse too; doing something random 'just because something about it appeals' can end up paying dividends later. The more I tune into my instinct the more authentic and rewarding my work feels.

Molly Gunn, entrepreneur and writer:

Because you're in your forties and haven't done 'it' yet, this doesn't mean you can't do 'it'. Whatever it is… writing a book, learning to sail, skateboarding, doing an art degree. Give it a go. You are not too old and it is not too late!

And finally, one of my favourite pieces of advice comes from Kate Hiscox, fashion influencer, writer and consultant:

> Be yourself. Don't try and be younger and 'cooler', aim to be respected for your experience, be that in life or work. Don't take any shit.

It's never too late and so whatever your age, wherever you are, remind yourself of that fact. And above all, maintain perspective. The advantage of being older is that we have amassed a huge amount of life experience. What feels like a massive obstacle or conflict at work will blow over just as it has done before. The sigh will reverberate around the universe and cease.

A new work dawn has come.

CHAPTER FOURTEEN

So, What Next? Working in Your Forties, Fifties and Beyond…

There are days when I feel overwhelmingly tired at the prospect that I will no doubt have to work for at least another 20 years.

There are days when I just want to give this work thing up.

But I can't because I need money. I also can't because I enjoy working and the structure it gives my life. I like it because it's challenging and when it's going well it teaches me new things and makes sure I don't get too stuck in my ways. It introduces me to people that I wouldn't ordinarily meet. I often can't be bothered and feel tired at the thought of it and there are times when I inwardly groan when I'm in a meeting and the same things are being said and the same mistakes made and it all feels too Groundhog Day. But I have worked all my life and don't expect to retire any time soon.

My dream is that work can bring me money but also some joy. I don't have massive expectations but there needs to be a good ratio of joy versus drudge. All jobs have drudge and that's just the way it is. I haven't met anyone who hasn't got some stuff in their professional life that they detest. You can spend your entire life looking at others and thinking their jobs are better than yours or you can make the best of what you have now and move towards the things that you enjoy more.

I take my hat off to women who can look after children full time but I need to work or I become unhealthy and obsessive.

I have had to recognise my limitations and put less pressure on myself. I cannot bake. I cannot pack a good bag for the seaside. I find the concept of camping overwhelming and I will always have a loft full of junk and cupboards that have shit falling out of them whenever I try and pull something out. When it goes wrong is when we try and do everything and be everything. There are only so many pots you can have on the boil at the same time. I've touched on this before but there is always an area in your life that will be compromised. The idea that you can *lean in* to all aspects of your life always will just result in your head flying off. I can lean in at work but that requires leaning out of parenting. I can lean in to parenting but that requires leaning out at work. I cannot have a fully rounded social life and be fit and healthy so I sacrifice the social life (or find exercise I can do with friends). I cannot be a hedonist and hold down a job so I sacrifice booze (it makes me paranoid and suspicious of colleagues). I cannot have one of those wardrobes with shoe boxes with Polaroids on the front and my trainers will always be full of sand. I will always find a Sylvanian family outfit in my trousers in a work meeting and cannot give up carbs because I need some balance in my life.

Work and life in your forties is about acknowledging what you can boil, what you can simmer and what you can simply chuck down the sink. This isn't defeatist. This is about self-knowledge. This is about realising that work is just one aspect of life and your involvement and engagement with it will shift and change as your life circumstances do the same.

I do not want to be Sheryl Sandberg but I respect her. I say to her – well done and keep going. I do not want to nail it or boss it. I used to think this was what I wanted and I wasted a lot of time trying to get there.

After the global pandemic that we've been through, we are all looking at our lives differently. It's an exciting time. We are still hungry for a new definition of work that is healthier, more flexible, more human, and one that is not purely driven by profit and short-term gains. There are, however, a lot of practical challenges, like creating affordable childcare, sharing the parental load, ensuring that we are more open about issues like IVF and the menopause. Talking openly about anxiety. Learning to be more direct when we are upset at work rather than sitting on those feelings and repeating the same mistakes. We need to actually be supportive of other women rather than just talking about it (and creating catching Instagram memes but secretly judging women and their decisions behind their backs).

Ask yourself what you need right now

At this moment, I need flexibility. I need some outlet for my creativity. I don't expect things to be perfect. I don't expect to not have difficult people or situations. I know that there will be days when I get anxious and days when I fail. The difference now is perspective. I have worked for long enough to know that what seems overwhelming one moment, dissolves the next. I also recognise the signs of burnout and can intervene early on to prevent it happening.

Age = experience = top job skills.

You have navigated a whole host of different situations and if you have been working or raising children or doing both or looking after elderly parents or trying to start up your own business, you have experience and it is this experience that is valuable to the world at large. The fact that you recognise stress when you read a client email and know that if you reply with the same tone, you will just amplify that feeling.

You are not a lack. You are experience. You are powerful.

Think about all those women mentioned at the beginning of this book. Think of all that wasted potential as women through the ages looked out on that horizon and thought about doing something with their lives but just didn't know what. I don't want you to feel under pressure but think about those women and then think about your own life. What do you want to do? Do you want more than you currently have? This is not about applying pressure because Lord knows we have enough of that already but it is about thinking, *Shit, I am in my late forties now and don't want to put up with this for a minute longer.*

Make changes where you can.

If you can't make them now, if you can't leave your job then start to look at ways that you can inch towards what you want to do. You might think about (if you can afford to do it for a while) going part time and spending some time developing the thing that you feel passionate about. Or you may – and this is often the case – not feel passionate about work, and that's fine too. Just make sure that it is not something that is making you feel miserable. Create boundaries. Tell work to fuck off but realise that there will be days that'll feel tough and you'll need to fight that inner critic.

It's never too late to learn new things. A while back, if you'd told me that I'd be working part time for an app, and managing their social media, PR and events, I would have thought that was ludicrous. I thought start-ups were just for young people. There are days when I still feel that way. I didn't know people my age could do that shit. The shift has been hard at times because in the beginning I had to Google just about everything (and that negative voice in my head kept telling me I was too old to learn) but I have just about managed it – no, I have more than managed it. I guess what I am saying is that there is still time to discover work that is enjoyable.

Fuck nailing it.

You're not a mum boss.

You don't have to get up at four in the morning to write a to-do list (unless you want to).

You are powerful on some days and tired on others.

Work is just one facet of who you are.

Think about what you want from it and plan for it.

Don't cower.

Don't complain.

It's tough some days. There are days when you'll sigh and not feel like it. Other days will be better. Some days might even be fantastic.

Wherever you are in your work journey, I hope this book has helped you rethink the role of work and feel confident enough to make the changes you need.

You are mighty and magnificent. Tell yourself this in the shower. With a flannel on your face or without.

Tell yourself this because it is true.

The 'Fuck Nailing It' Manifesto

You may have grown up in a time when work wasn't equated with joy. Remember that times have changed (thankfully) and life is too short to be devoid of all joy.

Work doesn't have to be the *one* thing that gives life meaning. Capitalism has taught us that success is about money and social status. There are lots of different definitions of success. Think about how you define yours.

Your relationship with work will change. There may be periods where you want to prioritise work, and then times when you can't and don't want to. There is no shame in taking an easier role for now.

Adopt self-care routines that make work easier. Try new things. If journaling works and clears your head then do it. If walking outside is your thing then do that. Find the tools you need to make you feel better.

Create boundaries. Be clear on when you can finish something and when you can't.

Work on any tendencies to people please. This is your work, your life and whether someone likes you or not is kind of irrelevant.

When you're catastrophising about a work situation, take action and do something. Pick up the phone. Ask for support. Worrying won't help the situation, only action will.

On fragile days, have a shower and place a flannel with something that smells good on your face. Tell yourself you are brilliant and can handle whatever is coming up.

Don't read profiles of successful career women unless they make you feel inspired. If you feel demotivated and like giving up, just stop looking at them.

Channel someone who inspires you. This doesn't need to be someone on LinkedIn. It could be a rock star. It could be a teacher you remember from school. Imagine them facing the challenge you're facing. What would they do?

Be magnificent. Or mediocre. Or just somewhere in between.

Let work be what it needs to be for now.

Fuck nailing it.

A LETTER FROM ANNIKI

Dear Reader,

First off, I want to say a *big old thank you* for choosing to read *F*ck Nailing It*. If you enjoyed it, and want to keep up to date with all my latest releases, just sign up at the link below. Your email address will never be shared and you can unsubscribe at any time. I know how annoying too many emails can be, believe me!

www.thread-books.com/sign-up

Why did I write *F*ck Nailing It*?

Well, put simply I was fucked off with work. Also, because of the idea that there was only one definition of work and that was one defined by capitalist patriarchy – the idea being that you dedicated yourself to work, putting all other things to one side and you'd be rewarded with happiness and satisfaction. Unfortunately, I'd tried this path out for myself and it hadn't quite delivered. In fact, it took me 18 years to realise that 'nailing it,' and 'bossing it' and 'winning' was a ticket to exhaustion, burnout and disillusionment. By the time I reached managing partner at the global market research agency where I'd worked for 18 years, I was necking painkillers to get through each day, crying if someone sent me an innocuous email, and wondering how come all these other bossing it CEO-type women were combining work with young kids, elderly parents, partners, having a social life, or in fact anything at all. I felt like a massive flop because I believed I'd failed big time at this thing called work. I realised that a lot of women were feeling similarly disenfranchised. Perhaps because they'd been on maternity leave and were unable to get back into the swing of work, or they'd worked in a toxic environment for so long they had no confidence, or they simply didn't know what to do next.

We are taught that work is pivotal, that it is the thing that defines us so if we don't thrive at work, we feel insecure and lacking. The funny thing is that work is important but there doesn't need to be one definition of success. In fact, there may be times in your life when it recedes to the background and you're basically doggy paddling, not really going anywhere (this has been me for a while) or there are times when you are acting out Tina Turner in 'Simply The Best' and you are striding about and perhaps you are actually bossing it (and can create a support team to help you get all the other shit done). Work needs to change to fit our lives and not the other way around. For too long we've let it dictate how we live, and what we prioritise. For too long we've sighed as we've stared out into the horizon and thought, *Fucking hell, is this what feminism delivered us?* The reality is that we will be working much longer (into our seventies?) and we need to grab the bull by the horns, hope the bull has horns made out of Playdoh and then shape those horns to fit our lives (sorry, the analogy doesn't quite work but you get what I'm saying, right?).

I get messages all the time from women who are stuck in jobs they hate or are too scared to look for jobs because they've been out of the game a while or have bought into the idea that there is some idealised role that will *bite them in the arse* and make everything hunky dory. I want this book to have helped you prioritise what's important to you so you can go after it. I want it to have given you tools to navigate all the mental fallout that comes with our work lives. I want it to give you hope that you can find a role that suits you or to feel content where you are because you know that it's not forever. I wrote it from my perspective as a 48-year-old woman, but it's relevant to women whatever their age. There are so many things I wish I'd known when I was embarking on my career. Such as how I didn't need to aspire to someone else's definition of success. How nobody was going to tell me take time out to prioritise myself. Or how we need to stop pressuring ourselves – it is okay to have periods in your life when you don't *love* your job. In fact, it's the reality for many.

The trick is to find something that you can do well, that delivers some highs, not too many lows and doesn't leave you wrung out like an old, grey flannel. There should be room in your life for other things too, like bringing up kids, seeing your parents, looking after your pets, looking after your body and mental health. It needs to be sustainable. I want this book to get a conversation going around work.

I'd love for you to follow me on Instagram where I often do IG Lives with experts on this and other subjects that impact women's lives. I also love hearing from my readers – you can get in touch on Instagram, through my Facebook page, Goodreads, or my website.

Thanks, and remember, fuck the idea of 'nailing it' – define what works means to you and get on with it. Well done. See, it's simple really.

Anniki x

 annikisommerville

www.annikisommervilleisworking.com

 annikisommerville

anniki72

RESOURCES

Here are some books and podcasts that will help you navigate work and your feelings around work (not all of these are directly work-related either).

The Art of People: The 11 Simple People Skills That Will Get You Everything You Want by Dave Kerpen (2016, Bantam Press)

Big Magic: Creative Living Beyond Fear by Elizabeth Gilbert (2015, Riverhead Books)

Dare to Lead: Brave Work. Tough Conversations. Whole Hearts by Brene Brown (2018, Vermillion)

Flex: The Modern Woman's Handbook by Annie Auerbach (2019, HQ)

The Freelance Mum by Annie Ridout (2019, Fourth Estate)

The High 5 Habit: Take Control of Your Life with One Single Habit by Mel Robbins (2021, Hay House)

If In Doubt Wash Your Hair: A Manual for Life by Anya Hindmarch (2021, Bloomsbury Publishing)

Life's Too F***ing Short: A Guide to Getting What You Want Out of Life Without Wasting Time, Effort or Money by Janet Street-Porter (2009, Celestial Arts)

More Orgasms Please: Why Female Pleasure Matters by The Hotbed Collective (2019, Vintage Digital)

Preparing for the Perimenopause and Menopause by Dr Louise Newson (2021, Penguin Life)

Radical Candor: How to Get What You Want by Saying What You Mean by Kim Scott (2017, Macmillan)

The Book You Wish Your Parents Had Read (And Your Children Will Be Glad You Did) by Philippa Perry (2020, Penguin Books)

The Worry Trick: How Your Brain Tricks You into Expecting the Worst and What you Can Do About It by David A Carbonell (2016, New Harbinger)

We Can Do Hard Things. Glennon Doyle's podcast: https://podcasts.apple.com/gb/podcast/we-can-do-hard-things-with-glennon-doyle/id1564530722

What I Know For Sure by Oprah Winfrey (2014, Macmillan)

ACKNOWLEDGEMENTS

To Paul, who helps me when I'm feeling negative and want to give up. To my daughters, Rae and Greta, who don't like it when I do anything on a laptop but have inspired me to want more out of life. To Mum, who I trust to give me good work advice (and general advice). To Dad, who I miss and talk to as if he was still here. To friends – you know who you are. And to work colleagues who weren't massive power-hungry arse-wipes and actually took the time to be supportive and constructive. And to all the women who sent in their messages and input for this book – thank you for being so honest and open and I hope the advice here can help you navigate work too.